WHAT PEOPLE ARE SAYING ABOUT

PAN: DARK LORD (
HORNED GOD (

As you read this, Pan is opening his strange eyes with those lucid, rectangular pupils, which give him huge peripheral vision. He is observing you very quietly. Look up from the page, look around. He is here, now. Believe what I say!

Also be aware that at this same moment there is an Inner Pan within your psyche who yearns to be aware of things from this wider perspective, who aches to take you toward the dark recesses of your mind, and the wild, tangled undergrowth of your unconscious. As you make your own antic path into the Wild Woods in search of the Great Pan, your nape hairs might prickle, you might see things at the new edges of your vision and strange realms might open up. If you have a frisson of fear – you are on the right path. Keep going. There is light and love there too, in abundance.

Mélusine Draco's book is filled with pleasing seeds and roots that she has collected from obscure, musty corners of the mythological and literary forest. Just brooding upon them ensures that they will be planted and grow in your consciousness, often in startling ways.

And if you ever find yourself on hilltops in Wiltshire and see an elegantly ageing and once-handsome chappie chanting: *'Io Pan, Io Pan, Io Pan, Pan Pan!'* then you're probably hearing me putting to good use the practical evocations she gives.
Alan Richardson, author of *Priestess* and *The Old Sod*, biographies of Dion Fortune and Bill Gray

A fascinating and interesting read packed full of historical and mythological information and knowledge. Draco has researched her subject well, illuminating Pan as never before. His mystique and folklore jump off the page and make you yearn to find him in the forest!

Draco is a well respected instructor in British Old Craft and she shares her wisdom in her many books on traditional witchcraft and magic. This latest book richly adds to her collection. A must read for those interested in learning more about the Horned God with practical exercises to enhance the reader's consciousness along the way. Enter the woods – if you dare!

Sarah-Beth Watkins, author and publisher at Chronos Books

Pagan Portals

Pan

Dark Lord of the Forest and Horned God
of the Witches

Pagan Portals
Pan

Dark Lord of the Forest and Horned God of the Witches

Mélusine Draco

Winchester, UK
Washington, USA

First published by Moon Books, 2016
Moon Books is an imprint of John Hunt Publishing Ltd., Laurel House, Station Approach,
Alresford, Hants, SO24 9JH, UK
office1@jhpbooks.net
www.johnhuntpublishing.com
www.moon-books.net

For distributor details and how to order please visit the 'Ordering' section on our website.

Text copyright: Mélusine Draco 2015

ISBN: 978 1 78535 512 7
978-1-78535-513-4 (ebook)
Library of Congress Control Number: 2016943148

A CIP catalogue record for this book is available from the British Library.

Design: Stuart Davies

Printed and bound by CPI Group (UK) Ltd, Croydon, CR0 4YY, UK

We operate a distinctive and ethical publishing philosophy in all
areas of our business, from our global network of authors to
production and worldwide distribution.

CONTENTS

I call strong Pan, the substance of the whole,
Etherial, marine, earthly, general soul,
Immortal fire; for all the world is thine,
And all are parts of thee, O pow'r divine.
(The Orphic Hymns)

Chapter One

The Power of Images

In Coven of the Scales schooling, Meriem Clay-Egerton always saw Pan as the Horned God...and the Horned God as Pan. This was a traditional British Old Craft coven that honoured Aegocerus the 'goat-horned' – an epithet of the Greek Pan – not Cernunnos, the stag-horned deity the Celts had brought with them from northern Europe. It should also be understood that although Coven of the Scales held firmly to the philosophy and opinion that all faiths were One and all Paths led to the same Goal, it did not advocate what is now referred to as 'eclectic paganism'. So how on earth could this ancient, pre-Olympian Greek deity find his way into the beliefs of traditional witchcraft in Britain?

What CoS did teach was the desire for knowledge and experience, regardless of source. Each new experience was, however, studied within the confines of that particular religion, path or tradition, but each new discipline was kept completely separate from the other. Only when the student had a thorough understanding of the tenets of each discipline were they encouraged to formulate them into their own individual system. So why, despite the fact that no other foreign deities were ever added to the mix of traditional British Old Craft, was Pan accepted as a facet of the Horned God so far from his native shores?

In Greek religion and mythology, Pan (ancient Greek: Πᾶν, Pān) was the god of the wilderness and rocky mountain slopes, of shepherds and flocks, woodland glades and forests, hunting and rustic music, and companion of the nymphs. Yet even the Greeks were often hard-pressed to know how to categorise this most ancient of deities who had been revered in his native Arcadia long before his name and cult spread to other parts of Greece.

Pan has no part in the traditional Olympian pantheon because, like other archaic nature spirits, he appears to be much older than the squabbling, fornicating, incestuous tribe that resided atop Mount Olympus. In the Homeric *Hymn to Pan*, however, where he commences his 'literary' career, he is identified as the son of Hermes (also a pastoral god of Arcadia) who fell in love with Dryope:

Homeric Hymn XIX to Pan

[1] Muse, tell me about Pan, the dear son of Hermes, with his goat's feet and two horns – a lover of merry noise. Through wooded glades he wanders with dancing nymphs who foot it on some sheer cliff's edge, calling upon Pan, the shepherd-god, long-haired, unkempt. He has every snowy crest and the mountain peaks and rocky crests for his domain; hither and thither he goes through the close thickets, now lured by soft streams, and now he presses on amongst towering crags and climbs up to the highest peak that overlooks the flocks. Often he courses through the glistening high mountains, and often on the shouldered hills he speeds along slaying wild beasts, this keen-eyed god. Only at evening, as he returns from the chase, he sounds his note, playing sweet and low on his pipes of reed: not even she could excel him in melody – that bird who in flower-laden spring pouring forth her lament utters honey-voiced song amid the leaves. At that hour the clear-voiced nymphs are with him and move with nimble feet, singing by some spring of dark water, while Echo wails about the mountain-top, and the god on this side or on that of the choirs, or at times sidling into the midst, plies it nimbly with his feet. On his back he wears a spotted lynx-pelt, and he delights in high-pitched songs in a soft meadow where crocuses and sweet-smelling hyacinths bloom at random in the grass.

[27] They sing of the blessed gods and high Olympus and choose to tell of such a one as luck-bringing Hermes above the rest, how he is the swift messenger of all the gods, and how he came to Arcadia, the land of many springs and mother of flocks, there where his sacred place is as god of Cyllene. For there, though a god, he used to tend curly-fleeced sheep in the service of a mortal man, because there fell on him and waxed strong melting desire to wed the rich-tressed daughter of Dryops, and there be brought about the merry marriage. And in the house she bare Hermes a dear son who from his birth was marvellous to look upon, with goat's feet and two horns – a noisy, merry-laughing child. But when the nurse saw his uncouth face and full beard, she was afraid and sprang up and fled and left the child. Then luck-bringing Hermes received him and took him in his arms: very glad in his heart was the god. And he went quickly to the abodes of the deathless gods, carrying the son wrapped in warm skins of mountain hares, and set him down beside Zeus and showed him to the rest of the gods. Then all the immortals were glad in heart and Bacchie Dionysus in especial; and they called the boy Pan because he delighted all their hearts.

Hermes took his son 'wrapped in the warm skins of mountain hares' to the abode of the immortal gods, where they called him Pan, which according to the footnotes to the *Hymn* is derived from the Greek word 'All' – and the hare has remained a symbol of pagan deity to the present day. It is also incongruous that in a culture that prized physical beauty, this long-haired, shaggy individual retained his popularity and, more importantly, his power, down through the ages. (Although, in the Roman era, Pan was often portrayed as a youth, without the goatish features except for a pair of small horns.) Perhaps because, according to the entry in the occult encyclopaedia *Man, Myth & Magic*, Pan's haunts are the woodlands glades, mountain peaks and rocky ways, and dense thickets with gentle streams where he darts across the landscape as a keen-eyed hunter, he appealed to the common man whose simple lifestyle he mimicked:

> The Arcadians themselves were famous as hunters and it was natural for their goat-footed god to represent an occupation that was so familiar to his worshippers. It was also natural for them to describe the herdsman god as playing his pipes in the evening when the sport was over...
> *Man, Myth & Magic*

On his dark side, Pan was also said to be the cause of that sudden and groundless fear especially felt by travellers in remote and desolate places, known as Panic fear. Herodotus recorded that when Phidippides was sent to Sparta to ask for help prior to the Battle of Marathon, Pan appeared to him and asked why he was no longer worshipped by the Athenians, but still promised to help them by instilling fear into their enemies. As a result of the successful outcome of the battle the god's worship was re-introduced to Athens; a shrine was built in a cave under the Acropolis, where he was honoured yearly with sacrifices and a torch race. Being a rustic god, however, Pan was not worshipped in temples but in natural settings, usually caves and groves, although there is a unique temple dedicated to him next to the river's source in the Neda gorge in the south-western Peloponnese – the ruins of which survive to this day.

Needless to say, Pan possesses all the conventional abilities of the Olympian gods such as super-human strength and longevity, shape-shifting, stamina and resistance to injury. He also had some mystical powers, especially those associated with music and dance, and its magical potency; not to mention a very wily mind, a raucous sense of humour and a shout or scream that instilled terror in the hearer. Like the shepherd he rested at noon, and disliked having his sleep disturbed, but he could also send visions and dreams in the heat of the noonday sun – i.e. lucid dreaming. It is said that he gave Artemis her hunting dogs and taught the secret of prophecy to Apollo. Ironically, the ancient Greeks also considered Pan to be the god of theatrical criticism.

Yet Pan's image retained its immense power when Greek myth passed into Christian myth, with Pan's cloven-footed appearance providing a perfect concept for the Devil in the eyes of the new, evolving priesthood. In ancient and medieval times the common people were taught by being exposed to holy images, and fear would not have been instilled in them by being shown pictures of the Olympian 'beautiful people'; particularly during the medieval period, when the Devil was conceived as having horns and a goat's hindquarters. Pan's activities are those of a giver of fertility; hence he is represented as vigorous and lustful – the latter being one of the Devil's bestial characteristics and a condition abhorrent to the Christian clergy.

None of these representations, however, appear to be based on biblical writ since the Devil's *physical* appearance is never described in any religious text, and it doesn't take a leap of the imagination to see that the image is conveniently based on the pagan concept of the horned gods that were common to many pre-Christian religions and cultures. Pan in particular looks very much like the images of the medieval Satan and it has been alleged that the early Christian Church specifically chose his image to discredit the entire, widespread Horned God cultus. A similar image also became the basis for Baphomet, whom the Knights Templar were accused of worshipping, and which was later portrayed in Eliphas Lévi's 1854 *Dogme et rituel de la haute magie* (*Transcendental Magic, its Doctrine and Ritual*).

Nevertheless, once an image has become firmly engrained in the cultural unconsciousness it is extremely difficult to dislodge. Joseph L. Henderson of the Jung Foundation described it as an area of historical memory that lies between the collective unconscious and the manifest culture pattern; having some kind of identity 'arising from the archetypes of the collective uncon-scious which, on one hand, assists in the formation of myth and ritual, and on the other, promotes the process of development in individual human beings...' These mythological motifs, or primordial thoughts, lie dormant until some dream, vision or epiphany brings them to the fore – and often with conflicting emotions between faith and instinct.

Likewise spiritually significant paintings created during the Gothic and Renaissance eras were complex, fraught with religious fervour and symbolism. William H. Hunt, an English painter and one of the founders of the Pre-Raphaelite Brotherhood, observed: 'When language was not transcendental enough to complete the meaning of a revelation, symbols were relied upon for heavenly teaching, and familiar images, chosen from the known, were made to mirror the unknown spiritual truth.' And a goat-horned, goat-footed 'god' often in his misrep-resentation as the Devil was a popular subject with artists of the time.

As David Freedberg remarks in *The Power of Images*, people are emotionally aroused by pictures and sculpture: 'They give thanks by means of them, expect to be elevated by them, and are moved to the highest levels of empathy and fear. They have always responded in these ways; they still do...' for there are advantages and benefits to be gained from such images. 'The Christian apologist is likely to distort – or even to invent – information about responses to pagan idols [imagery], in order to clarify Christian attitudes to [Christian] images and to prove their superiority.' For anyone who has always been pagan at heart, however, those roots are anchored deep within the earth of national culture and folklore to provide an unbroken link with the ancient past.

Because behind every myth, fairy tale and legend – hidden within the art, song and structures of those ancient times – is an encoded layer of wisdom, science and truth passed down through countless generations. In *Modern Greek Folklore and Ancient Greek Religion* (1910), John Cuthbert Lawson recorded the beliefs of the Greek people that have been passed down from ancient times, certainly into the early part of the 20th century.

> I assume only, without much fear of contradiction, that many of the popular superstitions and customs and magical practices still prevalent in the world date from a period far more remote than an age on which Greek history or archaeology can throw even a glimmering of light. If then I can show that among the Greek folk of today there still survive in full vigour such examples of primeval superstition as the belief in 'the evil eye' and the practice of magic, I shall have established at least an antecedent probably that there may exist also vestiges of the religious beliefs and practices of the historical era.

Lawson's entry for Pan (Panos) in the section 'The Survival of Pagan Deities' reveals a relatively modern folk-tale of a magic pipe given by Pan with the purpose of ridding the world of some of its evil men and concludes:

> But perchance Pan is not dead yet, or if dead not forgotten. And if this solitary modern story, if it be genuine, testifies to a long-lived remembrance of his better qualities, so in the demonology of the middle ages a sterner aspect of his ancient character still secured him men's awe.

We also learn that Theocritus, the creator of pastoral poetry, gave voice to a well-known Pan-related superstition when he made a goat-herd say: *'Nay, shepherd, it may not be; in the noontide we may not pipe; 'tis Pan that we fear'* because of the god's rage if woken from his slumber. According to Lawson, it was this superstition that influenced the translators of the *Septuagint* (the Greek version of the Old Testament) when they rendered the phrase, 'which in our Bible version of the Psalms appears as '*the destruction that wasteth at noonday*'.' By this phrase, Lawson explains, 'the memory of Pan was undoubtedly perpetuated; for in certain forms of prayer from the 17th century, among the perils from which divine deliverance is sought, is mentioned more than once this 'midday demon'; and a corresponding *daemon meridianus* found a place of equal dignity among the ghostly enemies of Roman Catholics.'

In *Viral Mythology* the authors examine certain 'archoenigmas' – common themes and elements in ancient myth, stories, and art, architecture, iconography and symbolism – in much the same way as David Freedberg in *The Power of Images* examined religious art; and Erik Hornung (*The Secret Lore of Egypt*) and James Stevens Curl (*The Egyptian Revival*) traced the ongoing impact of ancient Egypt on the modern West. They also make the observation that the problems with symbols and art is that they cannot always be properly interpreted since they are open to misconstruction and misunderstanding. That is unless the reader (or listener) has the key...or in the case of those with an esoteric mind-set who possess both lock *and* key, all that is needed is a drop of magical WD40 to unlock the riddle!

But it is Kenneth Grant's comment in *Hecate's Fountain* that explains why it is necessary to turn to the wisdom of the past if we wish to reconnect with the ancient power of a deity such as Pan in the present: '...this cosmic power [Pan] is popularly conceived of in a goatish or goat-footed form, the goat being symbolic of the lonely leaper in high places, i.e. the aspiration and consequent exaltation of the soul to high and holy places...another reason for its association in the uninitiated mind with terror and the Great Unknown.' Grant continues:

It may be asked, why then do we not abandon the ancient symbols in favour of the formulae of nuclear physics and quantum mechanics? The answer is that the occultist under-stands that contact with these energies may be established more completely through symbols so ancient that they have had time to bury themselves in the vast storehouse of the racial subconsciousness... The intellectual formulæ and symbols of mathematics have been evolved too recently to serve as direct conduits. For the Old Ones, such lines of communication are dead. The magician, therefore, uses the more direct paths which long ages have mapped out in the shadow lands of the subconsciousness.

And we *do* make contact with these different levels of consciousness or planes of thought. The idea for this book came through at 3am one morning and over the next few days, Pan manifested in all sorts of divergent ways, and the channels of communication were opened. Books not looked at for years suddenly caught the eye; vague memories from the past came to the fore; relevant information suddenly materialised and *Pan: Dark Lord of the Forest and Horned God of the Witches* was reborn. Or, giving the last word to John Cuthbert Lawson: *'Perhaps even yet in the pastoral uplands of Greece some traveller will hear news of Pan.'*

Magical Exercise

In Socrates' prayer from Plato's *Phaedrus* (c.348/347BC) there are echoes of a genuine appeal to Pan for safe conduct when going upon a journey in Classical Greece, which can still be used today as a protective charm...

Socrates: Is it not well to pray to the deities here before we go?
Phaedrus: Of course.
Socrates: O beloved Pan and all you other gods who haunt this place, grant to me that I be made beautiful in my soul within, and that all external possessions be in harmony with

my inner man. May I consider the wise man rich; and may I have such wealth as only the self-restrained man can bear or endure. Do we need anything more, Phaedrus? For me that prayer is enough.

Phaedrus: Let me also share in this prayer; for friends have all things in common.

Socrates: Let us go.

Pan has been the patron of many things during his long lifetime – of nature, wild places and woodland, of shepherds and flocks, hunting and rustic music, mystical powers especially those associated with the magical potency of music and dance, and theatrical criticism; he sends visions and dreams and bestows the gift of prophecy. If you would call on him for help in any of these areas, make your offering and begin your entreaty with the opening: '*O beloved Pan and all you other gods who haunt this place, grant to me that...*' and see what happens when *you* open up these ancient channels of communication.

Chapter Two

The Great God Pan is Dead!

The Romans identified Pan with Faunus, and Plutarch relates that during the reign of Tiberius (1st century AD) a ship was driven near to the shore of the Isles of Paxi, when a loud voice called out that the great god Pan was dead. The emperor ordered an enquiry but no satisfactory answer was found and it subsequently became associated with the birth of Jesus in Christian legend. An explanation has been offered that what the passengers on the ship overheard and misunderstood was a lament of the worshippers of a local deity, Tammuz/Adonis, while the annual obsequies were being celebrated. Certainly, when Pausanias the traveller toured Greece about a century after Plutarch, he found Pan's shrines, sacred caves and sacred mountains still very much frequented by worshippers.

Paganism wasn't officially outlawed by Rome until 365AD when Constantius II took the step of ordering all temples to the Old Gods closed and began a pagan persecution that lasted for two centuries; by 438AD an edict imposed the death sentence for all practitioners of paganism. During his brief reign Emperor Julian attempted to introduce religious tolerance and the restoration of the pagan mystery cults but, following his untimely death in 363AD, his mission failed and the persecutions began again in earnest.

As every sensible person knows, however, it is impossible to legislate faith out of existence and the worship of the Old Gods would have gone underground, as all religions do when faced with persecution. For the followers of Pan, however, it would have been business as usual since his sacred places would remain the caves and groves, albeit in more remote locations.

This idea of a sacred cave was, of course, nothing new and

some of the earliest cave paintings of the Palaeolithic period depict figures engaged in music and dance. Although the familiar stag-man is the most prominent horned figure, there are many smaller paintings of horned men on small objects of bone and horn. These figures are usually represented with the horns of a goat or chamois, and are dancing singly or in groups. It wasn't until the Bronze Age and Iron Age that these horned figures re-appeared, occurring first in the Near and Middle East, where the horns are those of cattle, sheep or goats. Belief is remarkably tenacious if existing in isolated communities.

In 1921, Margaret Murray published her first book on witch-craft, *The Witch Cult in Western Europe*. Already a distinguished Egyptologist with an interest in the anthropological side of archaeology, when she began her researches into witchcraft, she approached the subject from the viewpoint of an anthropologist. The book caused a sensation among academics and historians, and for the next forty years, the *Encyclopaedia Britannica's* section on 'witchcraft' belonged to her. In *The God of the Witches*, published in 1933, she enlarged on her theory that the Craft was no more than a native fertility religion with shamanic overtones, although she personally had no belief in the supernatural or its hidden powers.

Her third volume, however, reversed the scholarly acclaim and Dr Murray's theories were dismissed as the senile wanderings of a 90-year-old crank. *The Divine King in England* (1954) expounded some of Frazer's *Golden Bough* legends of the sacrificial god by serving up an impressive list of royal and substitute victims of ritual sacrifice throughout the ages; managing to suggest that nearly every infamous murder in English history could be laid at the door of the witch-cult! It is understandable that at this point historians felt that her judgement could no longer be trusted.

Perhaps now is the time to re-evaluate the content of Margaret Murray's first two books, because many of her theories weren't so far off beam, if not strictly accurate; and it should also be borne in mind that in 1921 when her first book was published, the repeal of the Witchcraft Act was still 30 years away. Even her detractors admitted that Dr Murray always had solid evidence to back her claims; but sometimes she was carried away into making assertions that were seen as 'unjustified and extravagant'. That said, her detractors were academics not witches, and there are a lot of genuine snippets of witch-lore hidden in the texts that are not usually referred to outside contemporary inner Craft circles. And as far as the sacrificial god theory of the *Divine King*...well, let's just say there are dafter theories expounded in some best-selling esoteric titles!

Dr Murray wasn't saying there was an unbroken line of religious practice dating back to the dawn of time, but she was suggesting that a considerable amount of sacred pagan symbology and metaphor harked back to the Palaeolithic, Neolithic and Bronze Ages and had filtered through to the 20th century. For example, Pan's sacred hare was also indentified with the Germanic goddess Eostre and the Norse goddess Freyja; in Irish folklore, the hare is often associated with the *Sidh* (Faere Folk) and other pagan elements. In these stories, characters who harm hares often suffer dreadful consequences. And there's the enigmatic image of three hares with conjoined ears, chasing each other in a circle with their heads near its centre. While each of the animals appears to have two ears, only three ears are depicted; the ears form a triangle at the centre of the circle and each is shared by two of the hares. This symbol has been traced from Christian churches in England, right back along the Silk Road to China, via western and eastern Europe and the Middle East. The hare remains a symbol of some British Old Craft traditions.

Of all the horned gods of the Greek mainland, Pan is the best known to the modern world. From earliest times his character-istics have remained the same: the long, narrow face, the pointed beard, the small horns, and the goat's legs. As Patricia Merivale observes in *Pan the Goat-God – His Myth in Modern Times*: 'The paradox of being half-goat and half god is the very core of his nature.' Scenes of his worship show him followed by a dancing procession of satyrs and nymphs, while he plays on his pipes – so perhaps he *should* be compared with the little dancing god of the Palaeolithic people. And, as Margaret Murray observes, it is highly improbably that the cult of the horned gods should have died out in Neolithic times and remained unknown, only to be revived before the arrival of the Romans.

> It is more logical to suppose that the worship continued unrecorded through the centuries... Such a cult [as Pan and Cernunnos] must have had a strong hold on the worshippers, and among the illiterate, and in the less accessible parts of the country it would linger for many centuries after the new religion had been accepted elsewhere.

Pagan worshippers *were* illiterate people, but since reading and writing was the province of the Christian clergy, many of those monks had access to the classical Greek and Hebrew sources from which to illustrate their manuscripts. According to Christian texts, by the 5th century England was practically converted, but three centuries later King Edgar (*Monumenta Ecclesiastica*) found that the Old Religion was more common than the official faith...and until the Norman Conquest, Christianity in England 'was the very thinnest veneer over an underlying paganism...with all its rites almost untouched'.

Much of what is generally referred to as 'the god of the witches' stems from what is known as 'Bible witchcraft' – the literal interpretation of Biblical texts. Dr Rossell Hope Robbins, of *The Encyclopaedia of Witchcraft & Demonology* fame, maintains that the Devil or Satan was the creation of incompetent clerics, for in the transliteration of the Old Testament into Greek, the Egyptian Jews of the 3rd century BC used the word *diabolos* for the Hebrew 'satan', an angelic entity whose function was to test men's fidelity to God. He was not originally evil, but later became so by 'mis-identification'. When the Greek Septuagint Old Testament was translated into Latin, *diabolos* became *diabolus* in the early translation, or 'satan' in the standard Vulgate text. In the New Testament, however, the Greek word 'satanas' was used to mean something totally different: not an adversary against man, but an adversary against God.

It is even possible to detect the origins of evil personified as a goat from the scriptures. The animal makes its first appearance in Leviticus when it was banished into the wilderness carrying the sins of the children of Israel – hence 'scapegoat'. Scholars contend that the original Hebrew had no word for scapegoat, referring to the sin carrier as 'Azazel'. Since no one knew who or what Azazel was, liberties were taken with the syntax and the goat became the representation of ultimate sin and Azazel was placed in the hierarchy of demons.

This catalogue of 'mis-transliteration' is small in comparison with the even more far-reaching repercussions of the *Book of Revelation*, or *The Apocalypse*. Although the text has long been the subject of vigorous controversy and even scholars from those early days questioned its authority, it is believed to be a Christian revision of an originally Hebrew apocalypse. The Church went to great lengths to develop the idea of a potent adversary of all that was considered divine – an earthly representation of evil person-ified, welded together out of plagiarised passages and spurious identities foisted onto older gods. Pan, with the horns and lower limbs of a goat, not to mention his lusty nature, was an ideal, ready-made arch-demon!

The task of many monks in the early Church was to translate texts from Greek and Hebrew into Latin, and among the manuscripts would more than likely have been the myths and legends of ancient Greece, including Aesop's fables where fiction masquerades as fact. We know from Richard Kieckhefer's *Magic in the Middle Ages* that when medieval writers wanted to cite examples of magic they extrapolated what they needed from Greek and Roman classical literature, which they interpreted as fact. Fables and morality tales were written down and adapted, devising Christianised versions of the same story. It was only a small step to re-cast Pan as a representation of the Devil. With his horns, hooves and shaggy-hindquarters; adding to his slanting eyes the strange horizontal, rectangular pupils of the goat, and lecherous behaviour, he *was* the perfect candidate.

And yet for all Pan's strange appearance, he has inspired great writers both ancient and modern to pen hymns and odes in his honour. The fragments of Pindar's *Ode to Pan* claim that:

> In any case, the god Pan was seen between Cithaeron and Helicon singing one of Pindar's paeans. And so he composed an ode for the god in which he acknowledged gratitude for the honor the god had given him; it begins: *'O Pan, ruler of Arcadia and guardian of the holy shrines... O Pan, ruler of Arcadia, companion of the Great Mother, the holy Graces' delightful darling...'*

The *Orphic Hymns* are a collection of 87 short religious poems composed in either the late Hellenistic or early Roman era. They are based on the beliefs of Orphism, a mystery cult or religious philosophy that claimed descent from the teachings of the mythical hero Orpheus. *Hymn* X is dedicated to Pan and reveals the reverence he still commanded even into the late Hellenic era:

The Fumigation from Various Odors

I call strong Pan, the substance of the whole, etherial, marine, earthly, general soul,
Immortal fire; for all the world is thine, and all are parts of thee, O pow'r divine.
Come, blessed Pan, whom rural haunts delight, come, leaping,

agile, wand'ring, starry light;
The Hours and Seasons [Horai], wait thy high command, and
round thy throne in graceful order stand.
Goat-footed, horned, Bacchanalian Pan, fanatic pow'r, from whom
the world began,
Whose various parts by thee inspir'd, combine in endless dance
and melody divine.
In thee a refuge from our fears we find, those fears peculiar to the
human kind.
Thee shepherds, streams of water, goats rejoice, thou lov'st the
chase, and Echo's secret voice:
The sportive nymphs, thy ev'ry step attend, and all thy works
fulfill their destin'd end.
O all-producing pow'r, much-fam'd, divine, the world's great ruler,
rich increase is thine.
All-fertile Pæan, heav'nly splendor pure, in fruits rejoicing, and in
caves obscure.
True serpent-horned Jove [Zeus], whose dreadful rage when rous'd,
'tis hard for mortals to assuage.
By thee the earth wide-bosom'd deep and long, stands on a basis
permanent and strong.
Th' unwearied waters of the rolling sea, profoundly spreading,
yield to thy decree.
Old Ocean [Okeanos] too reveres thy high command, whose liquid
arms begirt the solid land.
The spacious air, whose nutrimental fire, and vivid blasts, the heat
of life inspire
The lighter frame of fire, whose sparkling eye shines on the summit
of the azure sky,
Submit alike to thee, whole general sway all parts of matter,
various form'd obey.
All nature's change thro' thy protecting care, and all mankind thy
lib'ral bounties share:
For these where'er dispers'd thr' boundless space, still find thy

providence support their race.
Come, Bacchanalian, blessed power draw near, fanatic Pan, thy
humble suppliant hear,
Propitious to these holy rites attend, and grant my life may meet a
prosp'rous end;
Drive panic Fury too, wherever found, from human kind, to earth's
remotest bound.

Herodotus in his *Histories* (2.145) writes of Pan's ancient status:

Among the Greeks, Heracles, Dionysus, and Pan are held to be
the youngest of the gods. But in Egypt, Pan [Mendes] is the
most ancient of these and is one of the eight gods who are said
to be the earliest of all; Heracles belongs to the second dynasty
(that of the so-called twelve gods); and Dionysus to the third,
which came after the twelve...

The British have always had a penchant for folk-tales, myths and
legends, if not paganism in general, and by the late 18th century,
interest in Pan revived among liberal scholars; by the late 19th
century his image had become increasingly common in literature
and art. Professor Ronald Hutton in *The Triumph of the Moon: A
History of Modern Pagan Witchcraft* tells of how a group of 18th
century gentry, led by one Benjamin Hyett, organised an annual
procession dedicated to Pan, during which a statue of the deity
was held aloft, and people shouted *'Highgates! Highgates!'* [sic]
Hyett also erected temples and follies to Pan in the gardens of
Painswick House and built 'Pan's Lodge', overlooking Painswick
Valley. The tradition died out in the 1830s, but was revived in
1885 by the new vicar, W. H. Seddon, who mistakenly believed
that the festival had been ancient in origin! One of Seddon's
successors, however, was less appreciative of the pagan festival
and put an end to it in 1950, when he had Pan's statue buried.

In *Pan the Goat-God: His Myth in Modern Times*, Patricia

Merivale traces the literary homage paid to Pan from Arcadian to Roman times, examining the different nuances of his character in prose and poetry from the Arcadian and Roman to the Renaissance and Victorian periods, where we can see him as divine, cast in a more romantic light, sometimes benevolent and often sinister – not to mention inspiring ballet and music from the imagination of Maurice Ravel's *Daphnis et Chloé* (1912) and Claude Debussy's *L'Après-midi d'un faune* (1912).

John Keats' *Endymion* starts by painting a rustic scene with shepherds gathered around an altar to pray to Pan and continues with a festival dedicated to Pan where a stanzaic hymn is sung in praise of him:

> O THOU, whose mighty palace roof doth hang
> From jagged trunks, and overshadoweth
> Eternal whispers, glooms, the birth, life, death
> Of unseen flowers in heavy peacefulness; [235]
> Who lov'st to see the hamadryads dress
> Their ruffled locks where meeting hazels darken;
> And through whole solemn hours dost sit, and hearken
> The dreary melody of bedded reeds—
> In desolate places, where dank moisture breeds [240]
> The pipy hemlock to strange overgrowth;
> Bethinking thee, how melancholy loth
> Thou wast to lose fair Syrinx—do thou now,
> By thy love's milky brow!
> By all the trembling mazes that she ran, [245]
> Hear us, great Pan!
>
> O thou, for whose soul-soothing quiet, turtles
> Passion their voices cooingly 'mong myrtles,
> What time thou wanderest at eventide
> Through sunny meadows, that outskirt the side [250]
> Of thine enmossed realms: O thou, to whom

Broad leaved fig trees even now foredoom
Their ripen'd fruitage; yellow girted bees
Their golden honeycombs; our village leas
Their fairest-blossom'd beans and poppied corn; [255]
The chuckling linnet its five young unborn,
To sing for thee; low creeping strawberries
Their summer coolness; pent up butterflies
Their freckled wings; yea, the fresh budding year
All its completions—be quickly near, [260]
By every wind that nods the mountain pine,
O forester divine!

Thou, to whom every fawn and satyr flies
For willing service; whether to surprise
The squatted hare while in half sleeping fit; [265]
Or upward ragged precipices flit
To save poor lambkins from the eagle's maw;
Or by mysterious enticement draw
Bewildered shepherds to their path again;
Or to tread breathless round the frothy main, [270]
And gather up all fancifullest shells
For thee to tumble into Naiads' cells,
And, being hidden, laugh at their out-peeping;
Or to delight thee with fantastic leaping,
The while they pelt each other on the crown [275]
With silvery oak apples, and fir cones brown—
By all the echoes that about thee ring,
Hear us, O satyr king!

O Hearkener to the loud clapping shears,
While ever and anon to his shorn peers [280]
A ram goes bleating: Winder of the horn,
When snouted wild-boars routing tender corn
Anger our huntsman: Breather round our farms,

To keep off mildews, and all weather harms:
Strange ministrant of undescribed sounds, [285]
That come a swooning over hollow grounds,
And wither drearily on barren moors:
Dread opener of the mysterious doors
Leading to universal knowledge—see,
Great son of Dryope, [290]
The many that are come to pay their vows
With leaves about their brows!

And Percy Bysshe Shelley gave us his own *Hymn of Pan*:

From the forests and highlands
We come, we come;
From the river-girt islands,
Where loud waves are dumb
Listening to my sweet pipings.
The wind in the reeds and the rushes,
The bees on the bells of thyme,
The birds on the myrtle-bushes,
The cicale above in the lime,
And the lizards below in the grass,
Were as silent as ever old Tmolus was,
Listening to my sweet pipings.

Liquid Peneus was flowing,
And all dark Temple lay
In Pelion's shadow, outgrowing
The light of the dying day,
Speeded by my sweet pipings.
The Sileni and Sylvans and fauns,
And the Nymphs of the woods and wave
To the edge of the moist river-lawns,
And the brink of the dewy caves,

And all that did then attend and follow,
Were silent with love,—as you now, Apollo,
With envy of my sweet pipings.

I sang of the dancing stars,
I sang of the dedal earth,
And of heaven, and the Giant wars,
And love, and death, and birth.
And then I changed my pipings,—
Singing how down the vale of Maenalus
I pursued a maiden, and clasped a reed:
Gods and men, we are all deluded thus;
It breaks in our bosom, and then we bleed.
All wept—as I think both ye now would,
If envy or age had not frozen your blood—
At the sorrow of my sweet pipings.

Patricia Merivale also shows that between 1890 and 1926 there was an 'astonishing resurgence of interest in the Pan motif'. He appears in poetry, in novels and children's books, and as the eponymous 'Piper at the Gates of Dawn' in Kenneth Grahame's *The Wind in the Willows* (1908), providing the reader with one of the most evocative images of the Great God Pan ever written:

> ...saw the backward sweep of the curved horns, gleaming in the growing daylight; saw the stern, hooked nose between the kindly eyes that were looking down on them humorously, while the bearded mouth broke into a half-smile at the corners; saw the ripping muscles on the arm that lay across the broad chest, the long supple hand still holding the pan-pipes...saw the splendid curves of the shaggy limbs...

By contrast, in Arthur Machen's novella *The Great God Pan* (1894) we read of a horror that ensues when Pan is invoked into the mind of a blameless girl during a medical experiment in an act of *lèse-majestè* against the god. The girl awakens from the operation awed and terrified, but quickly becomes 'a hopeless idiot'. On publication it was widely denounced by the press as degenerate and horrific because of its decadent style and sexual content, although it has since garnered a reputation as a classic of horror, considered by many (including Stephen King) as being one of the greatest horror stories ever written.

Machen's story was only one of many at the time to focus on the Greek God Pan as a useful symbol for the power of nature and paganism. A novel by Edward Plunkett (18th Baron of Dunsany), an Irish fantasy writer, called *The Blessing of Pan* (1927), has Pan enticing villagers to listen to his pipes as if in a trance. Although the god does not actually put in an appearance during the story, his energy certainly invokes the younger folk of the village to revel in the summer twilight, while the local vicar is the only person worried about the revival of worship for the old pagan god.

Despite the attempted demonization of Pan by Christian clerics, there was an overall regret for the passing of the world of the Old Gods expressed in later writings, 'and to think that the heart has lost as much as the head has gained by the substitution', a sentiment strongly expressed by Wordsworth in *The World is Too Much With Us*:

—Great God, I'd rather be
A Pagan suckled in a creed outworn;
So might I, standing on this pleasant lea,
Have glimpses that would make me less forlorn;
Have sight of Proteus rising from the sea;

It is understandable with all these classical offerings extolling the virtues of the Old Ways that a 'pagan revival' was an event waiting to happen. Or as Thomas Bulfinch observes: 'As the name of the god signifies *all*, Pan came to be considered a symbol of the universe and the personification of Nature; and later still to be regarded as a representative of all the gods and of heathenism [paganism] itself.' (*The Age of Fable.*)

Magical Exercise

In England, rue (or herb of grace) is one of our oldest garden plants, cultivated for its use medicinally, having, together with other herbs, been introduced by the Romans, but it is not found in a wild state except rarely on the hills of Lancashire and Yorkshire. This wild form is even more vehement in smell than the garden variety with the whole plant having a disagreeable and powerful odour reminiscent of a billy-goat. In her novel, *The Goat-Foot God*, Dion Fortune had her characters plant rue along the path leading to the grove where they planned to invoke Pan.

Rue has been used in folk-medicine and spell-casting since antiquity. The ancient Romans believed the herb could protect the user from the evil eye; rue is associated with the planets Mars and Saturn, and Elemental Fire. It is also associated with Pan and the goddesses Hecate, Aradia and Diana. It is also one of the ingredients in the famous 'Vinegar of the Four Thieves'.

Four Thieves Vinegar is a potion used in various folk-magic and folk-medicine traditions, for the purpose of personal protection, the prevention of illness, the banishing of troublesome people, and the cursing of one's enemies. This specific vinegar composition is said to have been used during the medieval period when the Black Death was happening; it was thought to prevent the catching of this dreaded disease. Other similar types of herbal vinegars have been used as medicine since the time of Hippocrates, and early recipes for this called for a number of herbs to be added into a vinegar solution and left to steep for several days.

The recipe seems to have evolved in western Europe, around the 15th century, and there are many variations on how to make it. The common thread between all the legends is that there was a terrible plague in a village, and the only people who survived were four thieves. Each of them had contributed one ingredient to a jar of vinegar and garlic, which they drank and somehow survived the plague. Since they were healthy and everyone else was dying, the four thieves went around the town and robbed the empty houses. Eventually they were caught and sentenced to hanging, but they were able to escape the gallows by sharing their secret formula.

Use cider, red or white wine vinegar and add four minced garlic cloves to a jar with a lid. Traditionally, each thief contributed a single ingredient, so choose any four of the following: lavender, rue, rosemary, mint, sage, wormwood, thyme, or coriander and add to the jar. Allow the mixture to sit for four full days (some recommend placing the jar in the sun, others in a dark cabinet), but either way, be sure to shake it once a day. After the fourth day, it can be used in spell-work.

Chapter Three

Companion of the Nymphs

The wood-nymphs, Pan's partners in the dance, were the dryads, beautiful nymphs of the trees, groves, woods and mountain forests. They were the ladies of the oaks and pines, poplar and ash, apple and laurel. Others were hamadryades, trees sprung up from the earth at their birth, trees to which their lives were closely tied and while the tree flourished, so did its resident nymph, but when it died she passed away with it. Dryads were specifically the nymphs of oak trees, though the term has come to be used for all tree nymphs in general, while the hamadryades were the nymphs of poplar trees, usually associated with riverside trees and sacred groves. Like other dryads, they can all shapeshift from tree to human form.

The dryads of ash trees were called the *meliai*, from whom sprang the race of mankind of the Bronze Age; while the *maliades, meliades* or *epimelides* were nymphs of apple and other fruit trees and protectors of sheep; their hair was white, like apple blossoms or undyed wool. The *oreiades* were the nymphs of the mountain conifers. The old forests of ancient Greece were primarily found high in the mountains because the lowland forest had been cleared for farming. It was therefore natural for the Greeks to think of the dryads as mountain-dwelling. The *daphnaie* were nymphs of the laurel trees, one of a class of rarer tree-specific beings. Other nymphs included the *aigeiroi* (black poplar); *ampeloi* (grape vine); *balanis* (ilex); *karyai* (hazel-nut); *kraneiai* (cherry-tree); *moreai* (mulberry); *pteleai* (elm) and *sykei* (fig). Not forgetting the enigmatic *hyleoroi* (watchers of the woods) of whom little is recorded in modern texts.

All these various wood-nymphs were the female 'Companions of Pan' with whom he passed his days...and presumably nights, too, in pursuit of pleasure. Nymphs were generally regarded as divine spirits who animate nature, and are usually depicted as beautiful, young nubile maidens who love to dance and sing; their amorous freedom set them apart from the restricted and chaste wives and daughters of the average Greek citizen. They were beloved by many and although they would never die of old age nor illness, they could give birth to fully immortal children if they mated with a god. Nymphs tended to frequent areas distant from humans, but could be encountered by lone travellers outside the village, where their music might be heard, and the traveller often spied on their dancing or bathing in a stream or pool, either during the noon heat or in the middle of the night, or they might appear in a whirlwind. Such encounters could be dangerous, bringing dumbness, besotted infatuation, madness or stroke to the unfortunate human who chose to linger.

The satyrs were Pan's male companions, with horse-like features, including a horse-tail, horse-like ears, and were ever-ready for physical encounters. They were lovers of wine and women and especially obsessed with nymphs, as art and sculpture of the Renaissance, Neo-Classicism, Romantics and Pre-Raphaelites suggest. Satyrs acquired their goat-like aspect through later Romans fusing them with Faunus, a carefree Italic nature spirit of similar characteristics to Pan. Subsequently, satyrs became nearly identical with fauns, and commonly described in Latin literature as having the upper half of a man and the lower half of a goat, with a goat's tail in place of the Greek tradition of equine-featured satyrs.

As a patron of rustic music, Pan created the musical pipe of seven reeds, which he called 'syrinx' in honour of the nymph of that name whom he loved and who was changed into a reed that she might escape his advances. He also loved the nymphs Pitys and Echo, who also fled from him; the former was turned into a pine tree while the latter from that day on had a voice that could only repeat the last words spoken to her. In Ovid's *Metamorphoses*

Bk I: 689-721 Mercury tells the story of Syrinx; classed as 'a dangerously pagan work', this was a 15-book continuous mythological narrative written in the meter of epic, and remained one of the most important sources of classical mythology for the Christian clergy.

So the god explained, 'On Arcadia's cold mountain slopes among the wood nymphs, the hamadryads, of Mount Nonacris, one was the most celebrated: the nymphs called her Syrinx. She had often escaped from the satyrs chasing her, and from others of the demi-gods that live in shadowy woods and fertile fields. But she followed the worship of the Ortygian goddess in staying virgin. Her dress caught up like Diana she deceives the eye, and could be mistaken for Leto's daughter, except that her bow is of horn, and the other's is of gold. Even so she is deceptive. Pan, whose head is crowned with a wreath of sharp pine shoots, saw her, coming from Mount Lycaeus, and spoke to her. Now Mercury still had to relate what Pan said, and how the nymph, despising his entreaties, ran through the wilds till she came to the calm waters of sandy Ladon; and how when the river stopped her flight she begged her sisters of the stream to change her; and how Pan, when he thought he now had Syrinx, found that instead of the nymph's body he only held reeds from the marsh; and, while he sighed there, the wind in the reeds, moving, gave out a clear, plaintive sound. Charmed by this new art and its sweet tones the god said, 'This way of communing with you is still left to me.' So unequal lengths of reed, joined together with wax, preserved the girl's name.'

Shelly translated *Pan, Echo and the Satyr* from the Greek of Moschus:

Pan loved his neighbour Echo—but that child

Of Earth and Air pined for the Satyr leaping;
The Satyr loved with wasting madness wild
The bright nymph Lyda,—and so three went weeping.
As Pan loved Echo, Echo loved the Satyr,
The Satyr, Lyda; and so love consumed them.—
And thus to each—which was a woeful matter—
To bear what they inflicted Justice doomed them;
For, inasmuch as each might hate the lover,
Each, loving, so was hated. —Ye that love not
Be warned—in thought turn this example over,
That when ye love, the like return ye prove not.

While a rather lengthy poem by Walter Savage Landor relates the
tragedy of *Pan and Pitys*:

...Cease to complain of what the Fates decree,
Whether shall Death have carried off or (worse)
Another, thy heart's treasure: bitter Styx
Hath overflowed the dales of Arcady,
And Cares have risen to the realms above.
By Pan and Boreas was a Dryad wooed,
Pitys her name, her haunt the grove and wild:
Boreas she fled from, upon Pan she gazed
With a sly fondness, yet accusing him
Of fickle mind...

...It [a rock] smote the Dryad, sprinkling with her blood
The tree they sat beneath: there faithful Pan
Mused often, often call'd aloud the name
Of Pitys, and wiped off tear after tear
From the hoarse pipe, then threw it wildly by,
And never from that day wore other wreath
Than off the pine-tree darkened with her gore.

Pan was famous for his sexual prowess, and is often depicted with an erect phallus. Diogenes of Sinope, speaking in jest, related a myth of Pan learning masturbation from his father, Hermes, and teaching the habit to shepherds. Richard Payne Knight, a classical scholar, connoisseur and archaeologist was best known for his theories of picturesque beauty and for his interest in ancient phallic imagery. His first book, *The Worship of Priapus* (1786), sought to recover the importance of ancient phallic cults and discussed Pan as a symbol of creation expressed through sexuality. *'Pan is represented pouring water upon the organ of generation; that is, invigorating the active creative power by the prolific element.'* The central claim of the book was that there was a global impulse to worship 'the generative principle' that was promoted through genital imagery, and that this imagery has persisted into the modern age. It was an attempt to argue that ancient paganism had persisted despite the machinations of Christianity to stamp it out.

According to *The Gods of the Greeks* (1951), Pan's greatest conquest was that of the moon goddess Selene, which he'd accomplished by wrapping himself in a sheepskin to hide his hairy goat form, and drawing her down from the sky into the forest where he seduced her. Selene was the sister of the sun god Helios, and Eos, goddess of the dawn and unlike Artemis with whom she was often indentified, several lovers are attributed to her in various myths. Both Selene and Artemis were also associated with Hecate, and all three were regarded as lunar goddesses, although only Selene was regarded as the personification of the moon itself. Her Roman equivalent was Luna, the divine personification of the Moon who was often identified with Diana. There are echoes of this story in Charles Leyland's *Aradia, Gospel of the Witches* (1899), in which Lucifer fathers a child on the goddess Diana. Taking into account the passage of time, the conflation of Greek and Roman deities, and the confluence of the unholy trinity of the Devil/Satan/Lucifer it is easy to how this ancient Greek myth might have influenced the later Tuscan story.

The classic statue of 'Pan teaching his *eromenos*, the shepherd Daphnis, to play the pipes', has also added the question of homoerotica in its historical context, as it occurs in many representations such as classical mythology, Renaissance literature, paintings and vase-paintings of ancient Greece and ancient Roman pottery. Pederasty in ancient Greece was a socially acknowledged erotic relationship between an adult male (the *erastes*) and a younger male (the *eromenos*) usually in his teens. The *erastes-eromenos* relationship played a role in the Classical Greek social and educational system, had its own complex social-sexual etiquette, and was an important social institution among the upper classes.

Robin Osborne an English historian of classical antiquity, who is particularly interested in ancient Greece, has pointed out that:

...the English word 'pederasty' in present-day usage might imply the abuse of minors in certain jurisdictions; Athenian law, for instance, recognized consent but not age as a factor in regulating sexual behavior and historical discussion of *paiderastia* is complicated by 21st-century moral standards despite there being prosecution for a man violating a boy who was too young to consent to becoming an *eromenos*.

All this classical literature provided a yardstick by which the medieval Church could judge sexual deviancy – judging by the content of the *Malleus Malificarum* (1486) itself a catalogue of over-heated, Christian sexual flights of fantasy run riot – and no doubt introducing a few variations its clergy hadn't heard of before! In *Sex, Dissidence and Damnation*, Jeffrey Richards informs us that the Church took the lead in prescribing what sexual acts people might indulge in and regulated where, when and with whom sex could take place.

> For Christianity was from its early days a sex-negative religion. That is to say, Christian thinkers regarded sex at best a kind of necessary evil... Christ had said nothing about 'Original Sin' but in the second century Clement of Alexandria linked it directly to the discovery of sex by Adam and Eve...identifying [it] with sexual desire rather than simply sex... Original Sin equals sex...

By this definition *all* sex outside marriage was a sin, and inside marriage an abomination that stressed it was a mortal sin for a man to embrace his wife solely for pleasure. 'A man who is too passionately in love with his wife is an adulterer!' said that silly old fool, St Jerome. Needless to say, our old friend the Devil enters the equation and the Church associated all illicit sex with him and his demons, whose utter depravity could only be excelled by the lascivious thoughts of the clergy who invented them.

It was only one step from here to where sexual relations with the Devil and his minions lifted debauchery to a whole new dimension. As Dr Hope Robbins recorded in his *Encyclopaedia*, according to the confessions extracted from the Inquisition's victims by the courts, women attending sabbats *always* had sexual intercourse with the Devil; with theologians debating on the nature of devils and the extent of the sin, and the techniques of the act. 'The curiosity of the judges was insatiable to learn all the possible details as to sexual intercourse, and their industry in pushing the examinations was rewarded by an abundance of foul imaginations.' Thus, concluded Dr Robbins, a combination of prurient inquisitors and hysterical women about to be burned or hanged produced most of the accounts, which are completely the product of erotic and neurotic imaginations. Woodcuts of the time, used to illustrate the various manuscripts and documents and showing a horned Devil surrounded by fawning females, also bear a marked resemblance to the classic images of Pan surrounded by his nymphs. And, as it was observed earlier, it has been alleged that the early Christian Church specifically chose his image to discredit the entire Horned God cultus.

In his Introduction to the Folio edition of *Malleus Malificarum*, Pennethorne Hughes posed the question of why the great witch persecutions detonated when they did, and not at the beginning of the Church's history. The answer he gave was that in the early Middle Ages the hold of Christianity was so weak that pagan observances had usually to be adapted or tolerated.

In the first centuries of Christendom it was enough to demand a nominal conversion, and wisely to overlook the rites and beliefs of earlier religions, particularly if these could be attached to the name of recognised saints. Underneath the superficial structure of Christianity the Old Religion went on, with its feats and taboos... Thus the panic measures to stamp out witchcraft came not from strength but from an establishment facing despair...

In the meantime, in Rome, Hebrew texts were also plundered for details of the lurid carrying-ons of Lilith's offspring – the incubi and succubi. Even in the abridged version, the authors of the *Malleus* are seen to be citing classical writings to support their claims of evil-doing – to the extent of using Homer's Odysseusian shenanigans with Circe as proven fact (not to mention Medea, Canidia and Erictho described by Ovid in *Metamorphoses*). Circe was a predatory seductress, and her name in Greek, *Kirke*, is related to *kirkos*, which means a circling bird of prey, or a wolf. This suited the purposes of the Church fathers just fine and reveals the beginnings of the sexist stereotyping of women who allegedly practised witchcraft.

In *Sex, Dissidence and Damnation* (1990), Jeffrey Richards also points out that early Christianity did its best to absorb paganism, by taking over pagan holy days and festivals, appropriating pagan holy places and building churches on them, transforming pagan deities into saints. 'Even the horned and hoofed Devil of Christian mythology can be identified with the pagan god Pan... There were, however, certain elements of paganism that defied absorption, particularly fertility cults with their sexual rites and rituals.'

Overt paganism with strong overtones of magic continued to exist and to be fought against by the Church and state until the 9th century. As Richards explains, 'early medieval laws contain regular references to folklore beliefs, witchcraft and sorcery, though not, it has to be said, as an organised cult, and not as Devil-worship.' Jeffrey Burton Russell suggested that it was during this period when ancient paganism died out as an independent force and witchcraft emerged as a religious heresy like Catharism. Russell argued that at the same time as some religious dissidents turned to Catharism, others turned to witch-craft. As such it flourished throughout the Middle Ages, drawing its adherents from all sections of society.

In *Europe's Inner Demons* (1975), Norman Cohen takes a diametrically opposite view of witchcraft, but believed that intel-lectuals created a new and wholly artificial construct out of four previously separate and distinct elements: folklore, witchcraft, ritual magic and Devil-worship. The process of evolution was slow but by the end of the Middle Ages it was complete.

> People had always believed in magic. The ancient world used the term *maleficium* to refer to harm caused by occult means and applied it equally to witchcraft and magic... But this concealed the real distinction between high and low magic, between magic used for good and for evil ends. Witchcraft was essentially low magic, the folk medicine of the local 'wise woman', skilled in herbs and midwifery, but also able to turn her hand to love potions, poisons and abortifacients. It existed in the community, mainly among the lower classes, and was

practised by individuals and not in cults. High magic was a science, practised by learned men, involving formal rituals, books of magic lore, and the summoning of demons... Neither form of magic involved the worship of the Devil...

Cohen also showed how the realities of witchcraft and magic were grafted onto the fantasies that were part of age-old peasant folklore. Since Roman time there had been tales of witches (*strigae*) 'ladies of the night' with a supernatural leader, variously known as Diana, Herodias or Holda. These stories were then blended with witchcraft, ritual magic and the final and wholly mythical ingredient of 13th century Devil-worship, to create the now familiar stereotype.

Witch-hunting in England, however, was never as virulent as the persecutions in continental Europe and was probably the last great bastion of paganism. There were scattered laws against witchcraft, but as late as 1467, by which time thousands of witches had been burned in France alone, a convicted witch was more likely than not to have her ears publically boxed than anything more drastic! Inquisitional witchcraft came to England in 1563, much later than elsewhere, although there had been a statute against it under Henry III, it had been of brief duration. It was repealed by Edward VI in 1547 and only one conviction under this Act is recorded – and this was remitted.

Queen Elizabeth's Statute of 1563 resulted from pressure of the clergy, but it was during the Elizabethan era that literature moved out of the Dark Ages of sombre idealism and saw the emergence of pastoral and romantic poetry. The Elizabethan era also saw art develop from overtly religious imagery to the evocative and sometimes erotic when the artist reverted to classical allegory and the Old Gods began to again emerge from the shadows.

A Pastoral of the time, penned by Sir Philip Sidney began:

Join, mates, in mirth to me,
Grant pleasure to our meeting;
Let Pan, our good god, see
How grateful is our greeting...

While John Fletcher honoured Pan with his *Song to Pan* from his *Faithful Shepherdess:*

All ye woods, and trees and bowers,
All ye virtues and ye powers
That inhabit in the lakes
In the pleasant springs and brakes,
   Move your feet
   To our sound,
   While we greet
   All this ground
With his honour and his name
That defends our flocks from blame.

He is great, and he is just
He is ever good, and must
Thus be honoured. Daffodillies,
Roses, pinks and loved lilies
   Let us fling,
   While we sing,
   Ever holy,
   Ever holy,
Ever honoured, ever young!
Thus great Pan is ever sung.

This Renaissance brought about a period of intellectual expansion in art and culture, and witnessed a 'rebirth' of interest in the archaic past; a re-emergence of Classical subject matter, most notably the gods and heroes of pagan mythology. In *A*

History of Art, H W Janson, a former Professor of Fine Art explained:

> ...that the artist's outlook also underwent certain changes. Now longer a simple artisan and in the 'company of scholars and poets, he often became himself a man of learning and literary culture... As another consequence of this new social status, artists tended to develop into one of two contrasting personality types: the man of the world, self-controlled, accomplished, at ease in aristocratic society; and the solitary genius, secretive, idiosyncratic, subject to fits of melancholy, and likely to be in conflict with his patrons. It is remarkable how soon this modern view of art and artists became a living reality during the early Renaissance.

People travelled further afield and became familiar with foreign art where poetry and literature influenced painting and sculpture, and vice versa. When the artist gained admission to this select group, the nature of his work had to be refined: he was acknowledged as a man of ideas rather than just a craftsman. These liberal artistic concepts were defined by a tradition going back to Plato, and comprised the intellectual discipline necessary for the education of a gentleman of the time – mathematics, musical theory, Hebrew, Latin and Greek, grammar, rhetoric and philosophy. This was a veritable feeding ground for the creative artist who now had access to the works of the great Classical writers. It was also a time of great social unrest as Professor Arnold Toybee, explained in *A Study of History*:

> Breakdowns are not inevitable and not irretrievable, but, if the process of disintegration is allowed to continue, I find that it seems to follow a common pattern in most instances. The masses become estranged from their leaders, who then try to cling to their position by using force as a substitute for their

lost power of attraction. I trace the fragmentation of society into a dominant minority, an internal proletariat, and an external proletariat consisting of the barbarians on its fringes; and I sketch the social reactions of these diverse groups to the ordeal of disintegration. I also find a corresponding psychological schism in the souls of people who happen to have been born into this unhappy age. Discordant psychic tendencies which are perhaps always latent in human nature now find free play. People lose their bearings, and rush down blind alleys, seeking escape. Greater souls detach themselves from life; still greater souls try to transfigure life into something higher than more life as we know it on Earth, and sow seeds of a fresh spiritual advance.

This is a reasonably accurate overview of Elizabethan England and in its history we find a growing interest among the intellectuals in occultism and spiritual advancement, where some of the 'internal proletariat' – the spiritually dispossessed – became pioneers of regeneration; creating a higher religion drawn from native and ancient sources that offered an escape from the present to the myth-memory of an idealised past. The dissolution of the monasteries and schism with the Church of Rome during Henry VIII's reign also meant that the common people were also unsettled, despite the nationalistic fervour surrounding Elizabeth's ongoing war with Spain.

It was probably around this time that witchcraft began its own Renaissance. Shakespeare's theatre gave the common man the idea of witches influencing affairs of state; while Ben Jonson's Whitehall masques brought it home to the nobility. It is interesting to note, however, that Shakespeare's coven only consisted of three 'secret black and midnight hags' who worshipped Hecate, also that the song from the play: *'Black spirits and white, red spirits and grey; Mingle, mingle, mingle, you that mingle may,'* has passed into traditional witchcraft for casting the Circle. Both playwrights emptied the witches' store cupboard into the cauldron and hence the *'eye of newt, and toe of frog...'* has passed into popular imagination.

Fitting the mood of the times, Shakespeare's 'weird sisters' created an indelible caricature of witches, which has persisted in theatrical adaptations ever since. Taken at face value, the witches are doing no more than divining Macbeth's bloodstained future, but the Bard added to the political anti-witch hysteria by creating in his own inimitable fashion that *pot-pourri* of fiendish horror with which we are all familiar. Although much in dispute, the date given for the first appearance of 'the Scottish play' is generally thought to be some three years after Elizabeth's death, but the characterisation no doubt reflected the public image of witches from the few witch-trials that had taken place during the preceding fifty years.

Not so famous, but even nastier, were the characters created by Ben Jonson for his *Masque of Queens* (1609). The manuscript has survived intact, complete with Jonson's own handwritten stage directions; his reason for the anti-masque was due to James I having written a book on witchcraft and being obsessed by the subject. Jonson's cast consisted of eleven witches plus their Dame, who *'boast all the power attributed to witches by the ancients, of which every poet (or the most) doth give some...'*

...Homer to Circe in the *Odyssey*; Theocritus to Simatha in *Idyll II The Sorceress*; Virgil to Alphesiboeus in his *Eighth Eclogue*; Ovid to Dipsas in his *Amores*, to Medea and Circe in the *Metamorphoses*; Tibullus to Saga; Horace to Canidia, Sagana, Veia [and] Folia; Seneca to Medea and the Nurse in *Hercules on Oeta*; and Claudian to his Megaera in book one of his poems *On Rufinus*.

The Masque is littered with allegory and metaphor relating to ancient mythology, but there is no mention of Pan or any masculine god-form: in *Oberon*, however, the play is full of satyrs, elves and fairies (nymphs?) with only a fleeting mention of Pan in the text. We can, however, see where, when and how these ancient characters began to make their way into traditional witchcraft.

Nevertheless, painters of the Renaissance were also free with their interpretation of these classical images such as Titian's *Bacchanal* or Piero di Cosimo's *The Discovery of Honey* where naked nymphs and satyrs dance around the central figure of Bacchus. In fact, Bacchus (Dionysus) would have made a much better Devil as a corrupter of souls because he is a suffering god, who dies and comes to life again, particularly as a god of wine, who loosens care. His followers, the Bacchae, are shown dancing around him, tearing humans and animals to pieces in their intoxicated frenzy of possession. Bacchus, however, is usually represented as a pretty, rather effeminate youth with luxuriant hair; goats were sacrificed to him because he was sometimes perceived as a goat. His feast, the Bacchanalia, was eventually banned in Rome because of its degenerate orgies and excesses.

The Church, however, couldn't cope with a 'beautiful devil' and just as it had massaged the translations of the time, so it applied the same treatment to his image. Bacchus = satyrs and nymphs = Pan = goat-footed god with horns = Devil. The engraving *Satyr* and *Nymph* from the *Lascivie* by Agostino Carracci (c1590) shows the couple engaged in pastoral intercourse in graphic detail – including a smug expression on both their faces; while the engraving of *Pan and Syrinx* by Marcantonio Raimondi (1516) shows an identical horned figure about to pounce on a nervous-looking nymph. Graft a lascivious satyrian-horned figure onto a full-blow licentious Bacchanalian orgy and *viola!* – a coven of witches and their Master.

As David Freedberg observes in *The Power of Images*, little would be served by outlining the long history of the use of pictures and sculpture in private erotic context, from Tiberius's use of the most lascivious pictures in the rooms in which he held his orgies to the present day. The walls and corridors of papal palaces would have been adorned with such powerful 'classic' images and scuttling clerics would have passed them every day, so there would have been no dearth of subject matter from which to draw their inspiration. The suggestive, therapeutic and auxiliary use of these images, both high and low (compare the difference in impact of Giovanni da Milano's *Pietà* (1365AD) and the *Dying Warrior* (490BC) from the Temple at Aegina) extend abundantly into the present – and everyone knows of them from accessible galleries and museums from around the world. Good, evil, beauty and poor taste are always in the eye of the beholder.

There is evidence, however, that Pan also travelled with the legions in his guise as a fertility spirit, who became universally known throughout the Roman empire, including Britain. Evidence of Pan/Faunus being worshipped in Britain comes from the Thetford treasure that includes spoons inscribed with dedications to Faunus. By the late Roman period Pan would have been fully fused with Faunus, becoming part of the retinue of Dionysus/Bacchus. Many of the items in the Mildenhall treasure also display the typical Bacchic iconography of the late empire. The outer frieze of decoration on the Great Dish shows the god presiding over a riotous dance of maenads and satyrs in the company of Pan and Hercules. By the 4th century AD Pan had indeed arrived in Britain!

Nevertheless, as Dr Harold Selcon observed when researching the history of the legendary herbalists, the Physicians of Myddfai: 'Within the span of human time, recorded 'fact' can be suspect. So much is 'known' that isn't there. So much erased as 'incorrect'.'

Magical Exercise

There were constant efforts on behalf of the Roman priesthood to connect by means of ancient legends Rome's history and religion with those of Greece, and assimilating the old Hellenic deities into Roman worship. One example was the visit of Prince Evander of Pallene, a deific culture hero from Arcadia, who brought the Greek pantheon, laws and alphabet to Italy. Together with his mother, Carmentis, (really an Italian spring *numen*) he settled on the future site of Rome and there introduced the worship of Pan and the rites of the Lupercalia.

This enigmatic festival became part of the official Roman State cult, which more than all others appeared to have archaic magical elements embodied in it. It was celebrated on 15th February according to the Julian Calendar. The rites, which were acknowledged by the Romans themselves as being of incalculable antiquity, revolved around the central act of the famous running of the naked Luperci, wearing just a girdle of goat skins and brandishing thongs of goat hide as they ran around the boundaries of the Palatine Hill, striking bystanders and particularly women. The course of the Luperci around the Palatine is a *lustratio*, the making of a magic circle to exclude evil influences; the thongs cut from the sacred victim [Pan] convey his mystical power. The ceremony was described by ancient writers as a 'purification': it is a magical purification.

This festival is a more appropriate pagan observance for the 14/15th February than the nebulous St Valentine's Day, and can be celebrated as a homage to Pan, and to ask his blessings on the coming year (spring). Draw a protective circle around the home and sprinkle the boundary with consecrated water in an act of purification and protection.

Chapter Four

I Too Was in Arcadia

In *The Wind in the Willows* Mole asks Rat if he is afraid in the presence of the 'Piper at the Gates of Dawn', and Rat replies: *'Afraid! Of Him? Oh, never, never! And yet – and yet – I am afraid!'* Those who have grown up with Pan as a playmate would know exactly how Ratty felt at that precise moment. Back in those days it was possible for a young child to disappear into the woods with only a dog for company for hours on end without there being a hue and cry raised in its absence; and it was on those woodland rides and pathways – summer or winter – that I often encountered Pan.

The day would be peaceful and calm with a soft breeze whispering in the treetops, and the whole wood alive with bird calls. The woodland floor would be carpeted with bluebells in the spring; or summer sunlight filtering through the overhead canopy; crisp, dry leaves crackling underfoot in autumn; or the frozen quiet of a late winter afternoon as a fiery sun began to sink in the west, casting long shadows beneath the trees. Then, almost imperceptibly, there would be the sound of muffled footsteps following quickly in the undergrowth. Your pace quickened and so did that of your stalker. A suddenly flurry of old dried leaves would be picked up by a passing zephyr and flung into the air like a mini-whirlwind. All the hair on the back of the neck would be standing on end, heart thundering in the chest, breath almost impossible to take. Then you turned to confront this persistent intruder only to find...nothing. The wind died away, carrying with it the faintest sound of laughter and a voice in your head saying: *'Gotcha!'*

I knew this experience long before I was ever aware of who had been with me all those years ago, and he still catches me out from time to time. Out with the dogs in the woods or the lonely lane when there's no one else about, Pan will still be up to his old tricks. The long track stretches away into the distance; sunlight filters through the trees on either side and suddenly there's that sensation of someone coming up behind, ready to pounce. The old panic is there and you turn to confront...nothing. I've long since learned to laugh with him, but I can still hear that laughing voice saying: 'Gotcha!'

By contrast, *The Age of Fable* (1942) holds to the more generally accepted view that, 'Pan, like other gods who dwelt in woods and forests, was dreaded by those whose occupations caused them to pass through the woods by night, for the gloom and loneliness of such scenes dispose the mind to superstitious fears.' This is the evocative image Kenneth Grahame also created in a chapter called 'The Wild Wood' that conjures up the wood when it is feeling hostile towards any intruders:

> The pattering increased till it sounded like sudden hail on the dry-leaf carpet spread around him. The whole wood seemed to be running now, running hard, hunting, chasing, closing in round something or – somebody... And as he lay there panting and trembling, and listened to the whisperings and the pattering outside, he knew it at last, in all its fullness...the Terror of the Wild Wood!

There is a genuine, irrational fear of woods, forests or trees and the term hylophobia is derived from the Greek ὕλη *hylo-*, meaning 'wood or forest' and *phobo-* meaning 'fear', and many people do suffer from the complaint. As I mentioned in *Traditional Witchcraft for Woods and Forests:*

> The Wild Wood, however, is the dark, untamed part of natural woodland where unearthly and potentially dangerous beings are still to be found. This is not everyone's favourite place and

many urban witches never get over an 'atavistic fear of Nature uncontrolled'... On a magical level, the Wild Wood refers to those strange, eerie places that remain the realm of Nature and untamed by man. Ancient gnarled oaks, festooned with ferns and draped with lichen, carry an air of solitude and remoteness that is deeply unnerving—here birdsong and the trickle of running water are the only sounds to break the stillness. It is the Otherworld of the 'unearthly and potentially dangerous'. It is the realm of Pan and the Wild Hunt. In modern psychology, it refers to the dark inner recesses of the mind, the wild and tangled undergrowth of the unconscious. Here, among the trees, we are never sure that what we see is reality or illusion.

Pan's original stomping ground, as we know, was Arcadia – a vision of pastoralism and harmony with Nature. It is an allegory derived from the ancient Greek province of the same name, whose mountainous regions and sparse population influenced the term 'Arcadian' to become a utopian catch-word for an idyllic vision of unspoiled wilderness and bountiful natural splendour. According to Greek mythology, not only was this fabulous landscape inhabited by shepherds, it was home to the god of the forest and his court of dryads, nymphs and other spirits of nature. This concept also figures in later Renaissance ideals as a lost Eden and more specifically regarded as unattainable. The inhabitants were often regarded as having continued to live after the manner of the Golden Age, without the pride and avarice that corrupted other parts of the ancient world.

Arcadia has remained a popular artistic subject since antiquity to the present day, both in visual arts and literature. Images of beautiful nymphs frolicking in lush forests have been a frequent source of inspiration for painters and sculptors. As a result of the influence of Virgil in medieval European literature (see, for example, Dante's *Divine Comedy*), Arcadia became a symbol of pastoral simplicity; while European Renaissance writers often revisited the theme, applying the term to the spontaneous result of life lived naturally, uncorrupted by the march of progress.

Possibly the most famous Arcadian image, however, is that of the two paintings by Nicolas Poussin that have become famous both in their own right. *Et in Arcadia ego* is a 1637-1638 painting currently held in the Louvre, Paris, depicting a pastoral scene with idealised shepherds from classical antiquity clustering around an austere tomb. Another painting of the same name (also known as *The Arcadian Shepherds*), is by the Italian artist Giovanni Francesco Barbieri dating from c1618-1622 on display in the Galleria Nazionale d'Arte Antica of Rome. The painting shows two young shepherds staring at a skull, with a mouse and a blowfly, placed on a low pillar bearing the inscription: *Et in Arcadia ego* (I too [was] in Arcadia). Meaning that even in paradise there is death.

Thus did Pan and the concept of Arcadia remain alive in the collective unconsciousness: John Milton in his glowing description of the early creation in *Paradise Lost, Book IV*, alludes to Pan as the personification of Nature:

Universal Pan,
Knit with the Graces and the Hours in dance,
Led on the eternal spring.

Patricia Merivale escorts us on a wondrous journey through the world of Arcadia seen through the eyes of the poets (*Pan the Goat-God: His Myth in Modern Times*) who were inspired by this strange ancient Greek deity, whose very name evoked a lost world of pastoral settings, woodland glades and clear mountain streams. Wistfully they hark back to this Golden Age when the world was young and uncorrupted, but as Merivale observes: 'As many poets discovered, it is hard to imagine and harder to describe what such a god might be.'

Perhaps, however, one of the most evocative scenes in contemporary esoteric literature is the opening of Dion Fortune's novel *The Winged Bull* (1935), where down-at-the-heel Murchison, standing 'alone in the fog-bound darkness of the forecourt of the British Museum', cries aloud: *'Evoe, Iacchus! Io Pan, Pan! Io Pan!'* and a voice answers: 'Who is this that invokes the Great God Pan?' Murchison, an old army comrade, is a timely answer to Colonel Brangwyn's prayer – an Adept who is trying to save his niece from the clutches of an 'unsavoury figure with a penchant for even more unsavoury rituals'. Pan disappears from the story, but leaves a strongly imprinted although silent message that he *is* there for those who call upon him.

Dion Fortune also breathed new life into the god in the novel *The Goat-Foot God* (1936), and was responsible for many aspiring magical practitioners of the 1960s seeking him out for themselves. Gareth Knight describes the plot as follows:

> The leading figure is old Jelkes, who makes no claims to being an adept but knows his way around, having been a Jesuit novitiate in his youth before becoming an antiquarian bookseller with a sideline in occult books. One of his customers is Hugh Paston, a wealthy socialite who is toying with the idea of diverting himself with a bit of black magic. Jelkes saves him from this insalubrious course by introducing him to ancient pagan beliefs. This leads to Hugh sorting out some of his hang-ups with the help of the artistic and esoterically sympathetic Mona Freeman with whom he performs a spontaneous Rite of Pan in a bosky grove on an ancient site...

The late Michael Howard, editor of *The Cauldron*, freely admitted that it was Dion Fortune's fiction that set his feet on the long path of study towards ceremonial magic and traditional witchcraft. As Gareth Knight also pointed out, Fortune's approach to teaching occultism to a wider readership via the medium of the novel was a risky experiment and did not always come off quite as she'd hoped, but there are a large number of our generation who are eternally grateful for her guidance. Pan, once invoked, cannot be dismissed so lightly.

By contrast an invocation to Pan written by Aleister Crowley is a truly beautiful and powerful *Hymn To Pan* (1919) that painted the 'goat-foot god' in an entirely different light. Unfortunately the poem cannot be reproduced here for copyright reasons, but whereas Dion Fortune's writing was couched in the guise of romantic fiction, Crowley's Pan was quite a different animal altogether! *The Hymn to Pan* celebrates the god in a more Bacchanalian passion of raving, raping, ripping and rending to the famous refrain: *'Io Pan! Io Pan Pan! Pan! Io Pan!'* In *The Diary of a Drug Fiend* (1923) there is the instruction: *'You keep on saying, over and over: – 'Io Pan Pan!'. You go on till something comes'* – as come it will!

It is important to understand exactly what Crowley's image of Pan meant within the context of his writings, and we can discover this in the symbolism behind the Devil card in the Tarot deck. Together with the 'Death XIII' card, the 'Devil XV' is often completely misunderstood even in the present day. Eliphas Levi made an in-depth study of it because of the connection with ceremonial magic – his favourite subject – and re-designed the card, identifying it with Baphomet, an image associated with the Knights Templar. At this point in archaeology's history the nature of Baphomet was not fully understood, but at least Levi succeeded in identifying the goat portrayed on the card as Pan

In *The Tarot of the Egyptians*, Crowley explains that the card 'represents creative energy in its most material form; in the Zodiac, Capricornus occupies the Zenith. It is the most exalted of the signs; it is the goat leaping with lust upon the summits of earth. The sign is ruled by Saturn, who makes for selfhood and perpetuity. In this sign, Mars is exalted, showing in its best form the fiery, material energy of creation...'

In other words, the Devil card represents Pan Pangenetor, the All-Begetter and the esoteric references to the 'Night of Pan' (or N.O.X.), refer to a mystical state that represents a stage in the process of spiritual attainment. This playful and lecherous Pan is the god of nature, lust, and the masculine generative power, and since that Greek word *Pan* also translates as *All*, so he is a symbol of the Universal, a personification of Nature; both Pangenetor, 'all-begetter', and Panphage, 'all-devourer'. Ultimately, Pan is both the giver and the taker of life, and his 'Night' is that time of symbolic death where the Adept reaches a state where he transcends all limitations and experiences oneness with the Universe.

Therefore Pan can be found at Malkuth *and* at Chokmah on the Tree of Life. On the Devil card the Tree of Life is seen against a background of the 'divine madness of spring'; its transparent roots reveal the rising of the sap and before it stands the image of a goat, 'representing Pan upon the highest and most secret mountains of the earth'. At Malkuth he is the god of nature, regeneration and wild places; at Chokmah he is seen as the concept of pure spiritual force and fertility in its abstract form – the Great God Pan in all his glory. In *Magick in Theory and Practice* (1929) Crowley included a poem much more compact than the famous *Hymn to Pan* with the lines:

Do what thou wilt, for every man
    And every woman is a star
Pan is not dead; he liveth, Pan!
    Break down the bar!

An earlier member of the Hermetic Order of the Golden Dawn, Arthur Machen had previously invoked Pan in a much more malevolent form in his *The Great God Pan* (1894), but this was a novella of those meddling with things beyond their understanding. In the story, one Dr Raymond wishes to experience all that the world has to offer – this is what *he* means by 'seeing the great god Pan', but the experiment goes awry and with horrific consequences.

Here we can see that there is a marked contrast between the Pan evoked with respect and that conjured up out of prurient curiosity. And yet the 'spontaneous Rite of Pan' from *The Goat-Foot God* is no less powerful than the more terrifying outcome of Machen's approach. Even Aleister Crowley's *Hymn to Pan*, for all its intensity, still gives a sense of awe and reverence rather than terror. Perhaps the secret lies within the Great God's origins where, cut off from the rest of Greece by mountains, the people of ancient Arcadia could pursue their simple way of life, based on agriculture and herding, without interruption or influence from the outside world...

As John Cuthbert Lawson observed in *Modern Greek Folklore and Ancient Greek Religion:* 'We are apt to think of Greek paganism as a dead religion, and do not enquire whether the beliefs and customs of the modern [people] may not be a direct heritage from his classical forefathers.'

In the Arcadian tradition, Pelasgus was son of Zeus and Niobe, herself daughter of Phoroneus, the first human being. He was the first inhabitant of Arcadia and the first king of that country, teaching his people to build houses and to sort out useful plants from weeds. Arcadia owes its name to the mythological hero Arcas, another son of Zeus and the nymph Callisto; by his mother, Arcas was a grandson of Pelasgus, the eponym of the Pelasgians, a people living in Greece before the Hellens.

Lycaon (whose name comes from the Greek word meaning 'wolf') became king of Arcadia at the death of his father Pelasgus. Meanwhile, Callisto, Lycaon's daughter, had pledged to stay a virgin and was spending her life hunting in the company of the goddess Artemis. Zeus, having one of his customary shape-shifting, predatory urges, seduced her by taking the form of either Artemis or her brother Apollo and as a result of this coupling Callisto gave birth to Arcas and, according to some traditions, his twin brother – Pan.

Because Callisto had not kept her pledge of virginity, (or upon a request from that jealous old cat, Hera), Artemis killed her; Zeus, then, changed the girl into the constellation Ursa Major (the Great Bear) and entrusted the boys to Mæa, Hermes' mother, who raised them. Arcas succeeded as king of the Pelasgians; the country being then called Arcadia where Arcas was said to have taught his people to grow wheat, cook bread and spin wool.

Arcadia is a relatively poor and dry country in which it is hard to grow crops. In ancient times, it was primarily a region of cattle rearing, with herds of horses, sheep and goats, in which shepherds, under the protection of their god Pan (whose origin can indeed be traced back to Arcadia), occupied a leading position, unlike what was the case in the rest of Greece. Arcadia was also a country of marshes, in basins enclosed by mountains that retained rain water, which constituted ideal bird-hunting grounds. Despite the harshness of their country, the Arcadians were known for their mild manners and love of music, which may explain why they played a leading role in Greek representation of the origins of man. Yet, they were also good fighters and were in great demand as mercenaries.

Cities and Locations of Ancient Greece, Suzanne Bernard

Due to its remote, mountainous character, Arcadia seems to have been a cultural refuge, and Greek religion differed from the existing religions of the modern world in its origin and development. 'It had no founder...being a free, autochthonous growth, evolved from the various hopes and fears of a whole people. If we could catch a glimpse of it in its infancy, we should probably deny to it the very name of religion, and call it superstition of folklore,' wrote Lawson in his *Modern Greek Folklore and Ancient*

Greek Religion.

> Great centres of religious influence were developed, such as Delphi, exercising a general control over rites and ceremonies. But no single preacher, no priesthood, succeeded in dominating over the free conscience of the people. Nothing was imposed by authority. In belief and worship each man was a law unto himself; and so far as there were any accepted doctrines and established observances, these were no subtle inventions of professional theologians or an interested priesthood, but were based upon the hereditary and innate convictions of the whole Greek race. The individual was free to believe what he would and what he could; it was the general, if vague, consensus of the masses which constituted the real religion of Greece... Again in this popular religion, when it had emerged from its earliest and crudest form and had reached the definitely anthropomorphic stage in which we know it, we can discern no trace of any tendency toward monotheism. The idea of a single supreme deity, personal or impersonal, appealed only to some of the greatest thinkers: the mass of the people remained frankly polytheistic.

Our summary so far, clearly identifies Pan as a principal deity among the early Arcadians, a people who clearly 'played a leading role in Greek representation of the origins of man'. There is no indication, however – other than the fact that he has survived – of why this funny little rustic entity should have evolved into a mighty god of epic proportions from pre-Hellenic times right through the Roman Empire – and beyond. Other than the mythical paternal connection to Zeus or Hermes, both of whom littered Greece with their progeny, there is absolutely no clue as to why goat-footed Pan was far too important to be left out of, or marginalised in, classical Hellenic mythology. John Cuthbert Lawson's comments also suggest why Greek religion was so fluid and mercurial – and accommodating!

But even if the early Hellenic Greeks had only adopted Pan to keep the Arcadians happy, it still does not explain why the Romans found it necessary to merge him with the old Italian gods Faunus and Silvanus, and honour him annually in the important festival of Lupercalia. Unless...the name was believed to have some connection with the Arcadian *Lykaia* festival (ancient Greek *lukos*, meaning 'wolf'; Latin *lupus*) and the worship of Lycaean Pan; the name of the Arcadian king and Pan's possible grandfather Lycaon, also meant 'wolf'. In Roman mythology, Lupercus was a god sometimes identified with the Roman god Faunus...who was the Roman equivalent of the Greek Pan... Lupercus was also a god of shepherds...and his priests wore goatskins.

Evidence of Pan's early migration can also be found at Caesarea Paneas, an ancient Roman city located at the base of Mount Hermon, adjacent to a spring, grotto and related shrines dedicated to Pan, and an ancient place of great sanctity since the Hellenistic period. And why was it so highly significant that a simple pastoral god of shepherds was representing the deaths of the Old Gods with the strange cry: *'The Great God Pan is dead!'* – even if it was a misunderstanding?

All these fragments when pieced together begin to build into a convincing case for making the assumption that Pan was a much more imposing deity than we have been led to believe. Like a gigantic jigsaw puzzle scattering the pieces over thousands of years, an outline of the finished picture begins to emerge. One of the most intriguing pieces comes from Thomas Keightley's *Classical Mythology*, wherein he quotes the 4th century Latin commentator, Servius, describing Pan as:

...being formed in the likeness of Nature, inasmuch as he had horns to resemble the rays of the sun and the horns of the moon; that his face was ruddy in imitation of the ether; that he wore a spotted fawn-skin resembling the stars in the sky; that his lower limbs were hairy because of trees and wild beasts; that he had feet resembling those of a goat to show the stability of the earth; that his pipe had seven reeds in accordance with the harmony of Heaven, which was said to contain seven sounds; that his pastoral staff bore a crook in reference to the year which curves back on itself; and finally that he was the God of all Nature.

A letter from Symmachus, a Roman statesman and orator, to Servius indicates that Pan's champion was *not* a convert to Christianity. Symmachus, himself, was attempting to preserve the traditional religions of Rome at the time when the aristocracy was converting to Christianity, and led an unsuccessful delegation of protest against Gratian, when the emperor ordered the Altar of Victory removed from the principal meeting place of the Senate in the Forum Romanum. We can only assume that Servius was adding his own weight to the pagan campaign of protecting the sites of the altars of the Old Gods in central Rome.

Many centuries later, the choice of goat-like features for Baphomet comes from several connections between goats and fertility. Eliphas Levi himself called the figure Baphomet of Mendes, comparing it with what he believed was a goat-headed Egyptian god honoured for fertility purposes. While Pan, the Greek god with goat features, was likewise commonly associated with fertility in the 19th century. We now know that Levi got it wrong and that the 'goat' of Mendes was actually a sacred ram – a species of pre-dynastic sheep with long, twisted horns (*ovis longipes palaeoagytiaca*) that had been extinct for centuries.

The goat on the frontispiece carries the sign of the pentagram on the forehead, with one point at the top, a symbol of light, his two hands forming the sign of hermetism, the one pointing up to the white moon of Chesed, the other pointing down to the black one of Geburah. This sign expresses the perfect harmony of mercy with justice. His one arm is female, the other male like the ones of the androgyn of Khunrath, the attributes of which we had to unite with those of our goat because he is one and the same symbol. The flame of intelligence shining between his horns is the magic light of the universal balance, the image of the soul elevated above matter, as the flame, whilst being tied to matter, shines above it. The beast's head expresses the horror of the sinner, whose materially acting, solely responsible part has to bear the punishment exclusively; because the soul is insensitive according to its nature and can only suffer when it materializes. The rod standing instead of genitals symbolizes eternal life, the body covered with scales the water, the semi-circle above it the atmosphere, the feathers following above the volatile. Humanity is represented by the two breasts and the androgyn arms of this sphinx of the occult sciences.

Although expressed in the grandiose language of a 19th century occultist, there is a marked similarity in content between the later Levi version and the 4th century Latin scholar. Both are eulogising Pan on a much deeper, *mystical* level than is customary when referring to the little rustic Nature deity of the Arcadian woodlands. Nature, of course, has always been a powerful and emotive subject; Nature in its cosmic sense is a whole new, different ball game! Pan clearly has pre-Hellenic roots as his association with wild nature suggests, and his occupations were many and various, according to Alexander Porteous's *The Lore of the Forest*, 'whether he was roaming on the mountains, pursuing game in the valleys, or playing on his pipes in the groves, which music was often heard by travellers through the woods', there's much more to Pan than meets the eye.

As god of the wilderness and rocky mountain slopes: 'Often loud and incomprehensible noises were heard among the mountains and rocky places, which gave to the timid a kind of superstitious terror, and these being ascribed to Pan, gave rise to apprehensions which are now known as panic.' The wilderness is a wild tract or region uncultivated and uninhabited by human beings; or a mountainous area essentially undisturbed by human activity together with its naturally developed wildlife and usually hostile to man. Although totally inhospitable, it has been a place popular with mystics who go into the wilderness to confront their demons; while the 'scapegoat' of the Hebrews was cast out into the wilderness carrying the sins of the people.

From *Traditional Witchcraft and the Path to the Mysteries* we learn that although the uplands are generally inhospitable, there *is* an enhanced mystical sense of purpose to our journeying there. This is an alien landscape that makes us feel vulnerable and alone, but conversely we accept it with the realisation that having come this far, we *are* well and truly on the Path. We have endured and although the going isn't going to get any easier as we climb higher into the mountain, the ultimate goal is worth the sacrifice and danger. This is the experience for which nothing prepares us because we are conscious that whatever it is that we have undergone, the sensations will have been different for those who have instructed us – and different again for those who follow in our footsteps. During our time in this bleak, rocky wilderness we come to realise that if history leaves its imprint upon the physical landscape, it also *really* does leave an indelible impression upon the landscape of our souls. This is also a perilous place to be.

As god of woodland glades and forests: The Arcadians called him the Lord of the Woods and an altar to Pan was erected by the Romans in the grove below the Palatine Hill, but the woods and forests represent a buffer-zone between the past and the present, and for most pagan they were places of sanctuary and tranquillity away from the mundane world. There among the trees is a place of mystery and enchantment and so much of this has left its own footprint on our legends, myths and folklore. As that 1928 classic *The Lore of the Forest* tells us:

> To a wanderer in forest solitudes a sense of mystery is often perceived which lures him on and on into the verdant depths of the woodland world. On a brilliant summer day the tremulous throbbing of the air, seemingly full of whisperings and sighings from an unseen host, appears like the pulsation from the mighty heart of the forest, while, all around, sunlight and shadow form a tangled web of enchantment, which is deepened by soft elusive perfume floating on damp zephyrs. In fancy he may feel drawn back to the early primitive ages, when the forest deities would have had a very real existence to him, and he would understand the inner meaning of those oracles which were often spoken in the glades of the primeval woods.

This magic extends through every season of the year from the shimmering spring beauty of the beech woods; the lush tree canopy and cool shadows of summer; the rich tapestry of autumn to the winter when trees glimmer with hoarfrost. It has been said that the forest knows all and is able to teach all; that the forest, which always listens, has the secret of every mystery.

As god of Nature: Pan was the god of unmanageable Nature as well as pastoral landscapes and his companions were not quite deities, but not quite human either. These were creatures that inhabited the natural worlds of the forests, mountains, and waters of Greece and represent the untameable fertility of the forests. These woodland spirits took the form of men, but with decidedly animalistic features; similar to Pan with a goat's legs, a horse's tail, and horns or pointed ears. In addition, most satyrs sported exceedingly large genitals. Like Pan, the satyrs were frequent followers of Dionysus; uncontrolled revellers who sang, danced, got drunk, ran after nymphs and other females. This woodland realm was also populated by the silens, who were physically similar to the satyrs, but generally regarded as somewhat older, wiser, more powerful – and much more prone to drunkenness. They were experts in the arts of both music and prophecy. Possibly older gods of the forest, the silens also joined in the merriment of Pan and Dionysus.

As god of flocks and shepherds: Pan was frequently identified with other similar rustic gods such as Aristaios, an archaic shepherd-god of northern Greece, who like Pan was titled both Agreus (the hunter) and Nomios (the shepherd); as well as with the pipe-playing Phrygian satyr, Marsyas. In the actual region of Arcadia in the Peloponnese, Pan was the protector of herds and flocks, worshipped by the rural shepherds and farmers. The Arcadian myth drew in all these strands and was described by the Greek poet Hesiod (8th century BC):

> They lived like gods without sorrow of heart, remote and free from toil and grief, miserable age rested not on them; but with arms and legs never failing they made merry with feasting beyond the reach of all evils. When they died, it was as though they were overcome with sleep, and they had all the good things; for the fruitful earth unforced bore them fruit abundantly and without stint. They dwelt in ease and peace upon their lands with many good things, rich in flocks and loved by the blessed Gods.

The Greek poet Nikander tells of a shepherd named Terambos who was warned by Pan that a severe winter was coming, and advised him to drive his flocks down onto the plains. Terambos derided his advice and all his flock perished – the shepherd was turned into a cockchafer (a flying beetle known widely as a May Bug) for his arrogance.

As god of hunting: In Greek mythology Agreus (and his brother Nomios) are twinned facets of Pan; they are human in shape, but have the horns of goats. Both were the sons of Hermes, but from Argeus's mother – being the nymph Sose, a prophetess – he inherited his mother's gift of prophecy and his skill as a hunter. (Nomios's mother was the dryad Penelope. He was an excellent shepherd, a seducer of nymphs, and a gifted musician on the shepherd's pipes.) According to the Greek historian Diodorus Siculus (1st century BC), Agreus and Nomios could also be understood as separate nuances of the Great God Pan, expressing two different aspects of the prime Pan, reflecting his dual nature as both a wise prophet and a lustful beast.

Here Pan can take on some of the Gaulish traits of the Wild (i.e. frenzied) Huntsman that is common throughout northern Europe when we add the overwhelming element of fear into the equation. Although the dark forests, blackened northern skies and howling winds would be an alien concept to this deity used to the warmth of the Greek mainland. Pan's 'hunting' can be seen in his habitual pursuit of the nymphs *a la Bacchanal*, but his attentions leaned more towards the venereal than venery. Remember, it was also said that Pan gave Artemis her hunting dogs.

As god of rustic music: Pan was well known for his virtuosity and seductive talents using the deep, rich music from his pipes. This archaic wind instrument was most commonly played by shepherds, and representations of the instrument run right through the history of Greek art. Accompanied by the *tympanum,* a type of shallow, circular drum beaten with the palm of the hand, it was often carried in the *thiasos,* the retinue of Dionysus. The instrument was played by a maenad, while wind instruments such as pipes or the *aulos* were played by satyrs.

Coupled with the trance-inducing, rhythmic piping and drumming found in rustic or primitive music and characteristic of the Bacchanalia, it is not surprising that the senses became involved to such an extent as described in Euripides' *The Bacchae* – since music evokes strong emotions and altered states of awareness. This classical quotation from *Delphi* by Peter Hoyle, describes rites conducted on the mountainsides, to which processions were made on feast days:

> Following the torches as they dipped and swayed in the darkness, they climbed mountain paths with head thrown back and eyes glazed, dancing to the beat of the drum which stirred their blood or staggered drunkenly with what was known as the 'Dionysus gait'. In this state of *ekstasis* or *enthusiasmos*, they abandoned themselves, dancing wildly and shouting *Euoi!* [the god's name] and at that moment of intense rapture became identified with the god himself. They became filled with his spirit and acquired divine powers.

As companion of the nymphs: These minor female divinities often served as attendants to the gods, and Pan's personal entourage was made up of wood nymphs...typically described as those beautiful, eternally youthful and amorous maidens who loved to dance and sing. 'They dwelt in mountainous regions and the forests by lakes and streams, and although they would neither die of old age nor illness, they were not necessarily immortal, and could suffer death in various forms.' (*Haunted Greece: Nymphs, Vampires and Other Exotika*)

The ancient Greek belief in nymphs survived in many parts of the country into the early years of the 20th century, when they were usually known as nereids. At that time, John Cuthbert Lawson wrote: '...there is probably no nook or hamlet in all Greece where the womenfolk at least do not scrupulously take precautions against the thefts and malice of the nereids, while many a man may still be found to recount in all good faith stories of their beauty, passion and caprice.' (*Modern Greek Folklore & Ancient Greek Religion*)

Nevertheless, if the observations of Maurus Servius Honoratus were reflecting the Roman perceptions of Pan during the late 4th century and early 5th century, then there is the ghostly *suggestion* of a Mystery cult hiding in the shadows. The Romans were notorious for grafting every deity and Mystery cult in the empire onto their own rapidly expanding pantheon, and the durability of the Great God Pan's link with the annual Lupercalia comes down heavily in favour of the existence of such a cult. By its very nature, a mystery religion is reserved for the initiated only, and as all aspects of the rites remain unknown to outsiders, most of the Mysteries were lost with the decline of the Greco-Roman empires; modern knowledge can only be derived from sketchy descriptions, imagery and cross-cultural studies.

In ancient Greece, however, the Lykaia was an archaic festival with a secret ritual taking place on the slopes of Mount Lykaion ('Wolf Mountain'), the tallest peak in Arcadia. The rituals and myths of this primitive rite of passage centred around an ancient rite of cannibalism and the possibility of a shape-shifting, wolf-transformation for the *epheboi* (adolescent males) who were the participants. The nocturnal festival occurred yearly, probably at the beginning of May, according to W Burkert, who was a Greek scholar and author of 'Lykaia and Lykaioni' from *Homo Necans*.

At the summit on Mount Lykaion, Pausanias, a Greek traveller and geographer of the 2nd century, saw the ash-pile altar, but as attending the rite was impossible, he was obliged to 'let it be as it is and as it was from the beginning'. Near the ancient ash-heap where the sacrifices took place was a forbidden precinct in which, allegedly, no shadows were ever cast. Anyone who entered would have to be sacrificed. Modern archaeologists, however, have found no trace of human remains among the sacrificial detritus, although recent discoveries at the mountain-top ash-heap altar that Pausanias saw but was reluctant to pry into, reveal that it was much older than even the Classical Greeks themselves realised; pottery shards were recovered revealing that the site was in unbroken use to the Hellenistic period.

A sanctuary of Pan was also located upon the mountain. According to tradition, Euandros, that son of Hermes who led his colony from Arcadia into Italy and built a town on the Palatine

Hill, introduced the cult of Pan Lýkaios and the festival of the Lykaia; which later became the major Roman festival of Lupercalia (*Description of Greece*, Pauanias). All of these, in pulling all these strands together, add to the undertones of an ancient Mystery cult connected to Pan.

Patricia Merivale's concluding scholarly remarks in *Pan the Goat-God: His Myth in Modern Times* are also interesting:

> Such a Pan can be merely the touch of local colour in an Arcadian description, or he can be the universal transcendental Nature in which man ought to acknowledge his membership. If Pan is simply All there is, he becomes the subject of mystery cult, of philosophical rather than literary contemplation. Yet a central role for Pan in modern literature is as the object of mystic visions, Satanic or beatific, which pays feeble tribute to 'the dark presence of the otherness that lies beyond the boundaries of man's conscious mind'.

Magical Exercise

In *The Religion of Ancient Roman* there is a formal prayer of a Latin farmer, which has all the hallmarks of a magical evocation on the occasion of the *Parilia*, the shepherd's festival of 21st April when he begs forgiveness for any unwitting transgressions:

> *If I have fed my flocks on holy ground or sat beneath a holy tree, or my sheep unwittingly have grazed on graves; if I have entered a forbidden grove, or nymphs or the half-goat god have had to flee from my sight; if my pruning knife has robbed a sacred clearing of some dark bough, to give a basket of leaves to some sick sheep; grant pardon for my fault, nor let it harm me to have driven my flock in a hail storm beneath some country shrine...*

In *The Roman Festivals of the Period of the Republic* (1899) Ward W Fowler tells us that the sheep pens were decorated with green branches and a wreath hung on the gate and at dawn's first light the shepherd would purify the sheep by sweeping the pen and constructing a bonfire of straw, olive branches, laurel, and sulphur. The noises produced by this burning combination were interpreted as a beneficial omen as the shepherd jumped through the flames driving the sheep before him. After making offerings of millet, cakes, and milk, the shepherd would wet his hands with dew, face the east, and repeat the prayer four times to ask that the shepherd and his flock would be freed from evils brought about by accidental wrongdoings (e.g. trespassing on sacred grounds and removing water from a sacred water source). The final part of the festival consisted of the drinking of the beverage *burranica*, a combination of milk and *sapa* (boiled wine), after which the shepherd would leap through the fire three times, bringing an end to the ceremony.

This evocation is a pagan version very similar to the much later 'act of contrition' that can be used in connection with an examination of conscience: *'Lord, I am heartily sorry if I have offended Thee...'* We are looking here at a spiritual cleansing taking place before a general spring cleansing of the hearth and home with similar overtones to the traditional Beltaine festival.

Chapter Five

God of the Witches

Aradia, or the Gospel of the Witches was compiled by the American folklorist Charles Godfrey Leland and published in 1899, containing what was purported to be a genuine glimpse into the world of Tuscan witchcraft. It contained what he believed was the religious text of a group of Italian witches who documented their beliefs and rituals, although various historians and folklorists have long disputed the existence of such a group. Scholars are divided, with some dismissing Leland's assertion regarding the origins of the manuscript, and others arguing for its authenticity as a unique documentation of folk beliefs.

Aradia begins with the tale of Aradia's birth to Diana (aka Artemis/Selene) and Lucifer (aka the Devil/Satan/Pan), who is described as 'the god of the Sun and of the Moon, the god of Light (Splendour), who was so proud of his beauty, and who for his pride was driven from Paradise'. Diana instructed Aradia to *'go to earth below / To be a teacher unto women and men / Who fain would study witchcraft'*. When Aradia descended, she became the first of all witches, and promised her followers that: *'Ye shall all be freed from slavery, / And so ye shall be free in everything.'*

Diana was the Roman equivalent of her Greek counterpart, Artemis (Arcadian: Kallisto), goddess of the hunt, the dark, moon, the light, wild animals, nature, wilderness, childbirth, virginity, fertility, young girls and health, and plague in women and childhood – also known as 'the shadows of the night' and her cult was a survival of very old totemic and shamanic rituals. Selene was an early Greek moon goddess and sister to Helios, the sun god; in classical times the pair were fused with Artemis and Apollo. *Aradia* opens with the words:

Diana greatly loved her brother Lucifer, the God of the Sun and of the Moon, the God of Light (Splendor), who was so proud of his beauty, and who for his pride was driven from paradise. Diana had by her brother a daughter, to whom they gave the name of Aradia (i.e. Herodias)...

Lucifer, however, occurs only once in the Hebrew Bible and means 'shining one or light bearer'. The Greek Septuagint renders the name as Heōsphoros, literally 'bringer of dawn' for the morning star. The word taken from the Latin Vulgate translates Lucifer as meaning 'the morning star, the planet Venus', or, as an adjective, 'light-bringing'. With all this juggling with semantics, cultural identities and transliterations it's not surprising that the ladies of Tuscany (if they ever existed) got confused with the casting; but it is possible that the basis for the original story came from the Greek legend of Pan seducing the moon-goddess Selene. In itself, *Aradia* is not a convincing document, but among Leland's notes there are numerous references that refer to genuine Old Craft that would not have been readily available c1899 without some access to genuine witches.

Much the same reasoning applies to Margaret Murray's *The Witch-Cult in Western Europe* (1921) and *The God of the Witches* (1931). A thorough and careful study of the witch-trials in Britain convinced her that witchcraft *was* a survival of a pre-Christian religion, which she called Dianic. No one, prior to her researches, had gone carefully through the reports of the trials, analysing the descriptions of the rites and ceremonies, and of the organisation of the covens. As Nigel Aldcroft Jackson says in *Call of the Horned Piper*:

Her examination of the heathen nature of witchcraft was pioneering in its nature and she proved clearly that this was an ancient religion that had survived into the dawn of the modern era. *She erred in underestimating the visionary and*

> *shamanic nature of witch-spirituality and exaggerated the organisa-*
> *tional and congregational side of the Craft as a secret network*
> [author's italics MD], but she led the way for further develop-
> ments...

Agreed Dr Murray made some poor-judgement calls on occasion, but again the tell-tale signs are there in the text to tell us she had indeed been recording genuine input during her research. We all know the witch-trials produced some amazing fiction, but this aging archaeologist managed to record for posterity a lot of 'hidden' information that she probably didn't understand herself. Nevertheless, she recorded that the Horned God of Craft was a development of the many horned deities that flourished in the early legends of the Aegean throughout the Bronze and Iron Ages, and had had its way to Britain:

> The earliest record of the masked and horned man in England
> is in the *Liber Poenitentialis* of Theodore, Archbishop of
> Canterbury from 668-690. ...The worshippers [witches]
> themselves were illiterate and have left no records of their
> beliefs except in a few survivals here and there...

Everyone is familiar with the ecological term 'wildlife corridor' – a road or canal system that enables birds and animals to move from the countryside to re-populate inner towns and cities. Historically, a similar comparison can be made with the Roman legions that provided a corridor of migration for belief to spread throughout the Empire – among their personal belongings and in the baggage train, images of their gods travelled with them. For example: the Celtic horse-goddess Epona was adopted by the auxiliaries in the Roman cavalry, while even into the early Christian era, Mithras was the chosen god of the legions. The mercenaries from Gaul had certain deities, which virtually every Gallic person worshipped, as well as clan and household gods.

Many of the major gods were related to Greek deities; the primary god worshipped at the time of the arrival of Julius Caesar was Teutates, the Gallic equivalent of Mercury. Eostre was the German goddess of spring; and the 'Mothers' (Matres or Matronae) from Gaul were widely worshipped in a triple form, similar to the triple manifestation of Hecate.

It was only when Rome expanded her empire that any written record was made of the gods of north-western Europe, and those records prove that a horned deity, who the Romans listed as Cernunnos, was one of the great gods of Gaul. He has a man's head and wears stag's antlers; like his Palaeolithic prototype he is bearded. Although this Celtic god is most often referred to by modern commentators as Cernunnos, and equated with a horned deity often depicted sitting cross-legged and wearing a torc, Cernunnos was not a native deity to Britain. As the authors of *Roman Britain* point out: 'It should perhaps be stressed that the name Cernunnos occurs only on a single incomplete inscription from Paris' – but images of horned gods occur in Roman Britain, which archaeologists suggest were the symbolic male side of a basic fertility cult.

There is also ample evidence for Bacchic cults in Britain, especially in the late Roman period when they became a central element in the opposition to Christianity. Pan was one of the participants in the Bacchic *thiasos*; and such evidence is important, as it underlines the fact that this major empire-wide religion had a following among the Romano-British (*Roman Britain*). Bacchus was the Roman god of agriculture and wine (equated with Dionysus the Greek god of frenzies, festivities, spiritual ecstasy and wine). He is usually depicted as a pretty, effeminate, long-haired youth carrying a *thyrsus*, a wand or staff of giant fennel covered with ivy, vines and leaves, sometimes wound with a *taeniae* (ribbon) and always topped with a pine cone.

The Celtic Cocidius was sometimes combined with the Roman

god Silvanus, a deity of woodland and hunting and often associated with Pan/Faunus. Silvanus also had a canine hunting companion. These Celtic elements can also be detected in Mercury, often shown as a horned god, with a female consort, the goddess Rosmerta or Maia with her cauldron. So, was this how Pan first became integrated with early European witchcraft? Details and images of these foreign 'imports' were sketchy to say the least, but Pan had a popular and ancient lineage that had already been well recorded in literature and art for centuries.

There could, however, have been other reasons...

Firstly, early trading interaction between the Mediterranean and Britain was much more common than even the historians of Margaret Murray's day realised. With the religious persecution going full throttle under the Romans, many pagan sympathisers would be looking for places of safety, and when people migrate they take their beliefs and customs with them. The Great God Pan wasn't dead, perhaps he merely moved on with those who still believed in him; just as the Olympian Greeks and Romans had assimilated him into their own pantheons – and because he was too powerful to discard.

Secondly, it is doubtful whether Pan was really 'introduced' to the ancient Britons – because he had been here all along. We now understand that since Pan is only one facet of the 'Horned God of the Witches', those living in wild and wooded areas would have encountered him without realising it. The indigenous people would have been familiar with that overwhelming sense of fear that suddenly assailed them in remote and densely forested places: the Romans merely put a name and face to that fear.

A rather distant, hazy picture slowly begins to emerge from the past, and these images were probably the first time native British people had seen actual *physical* representations of their 'horned gods' and 'mother-goddesses'. These early shamanic practices were oral traditions and apart from the crude images from the Palaeolithic and Neolithic periods, the descriptions would have been handed down in songs and stories. This newly arrived art form would have been like comparing the matchstick figures of L S Lowry to the statues of Michelangelo.

The one that thing can be said in favour of the early Church fathers is that they were not stupid people; they were learned men and turned that power to their own advantage. Rome had benefited from the avarice of the emperors and was stacked to the gunnels with stolen art, classical literature and writings that were plundered with impunity to further the Christian cause. The Old Gods were converted into saints; holy days and festivals merged with the Church calendar; and sacred sites incorporated into the fabric of a new church. The birth of Mithras, witnessed by shepherds on 25th December, was appropriated to strengthen the Christian mythos, while various 'miracles' performed by the Old Gods were re-invented and re-branded with a Christian spin. Even the words of Homer were frequently grafted onto Christian stock!

Using the same sources, the Church fathers also had enough material to create a whole new testament of evil from those classical writings. Pan and his nubile nymphs cavorting in the wake of the Bacchanalia provided the basis for a witches' sabbat; men adopting an animal disguise to ravage the female attendees – Inquisitional records show the unnatural degree of interest the examiners took in hearing about the sexual activities of the Devil and his minions. Judging from the large amount of graphic designs on Greek pottery and Roman statuary there was enough visual material there to blow their ecclesiastical socks off! Even the most chaste of women would have been only too glad to confess to having sex with the Devil standing up in a hammock, in order to stop the torture.

Classical sources testifying to causing adverse weather conditions, illness in cattle and impotency were all charges laid at the witches' door and dutifully recorded by those two dirty Dominicans, Kramer and Sprenger, for their 'definitive work of diabolistic misinformation' – the *Malleus Maleficarum*. Animals usually identified with Greek and Roman deities now officially became witches' familiars – Aphrodite's frog; Hecate's toad; Pan's hare or Diana's cat – and if the accused had none of these creatures around her, 'the judges usually discovered a bee or fly or mouse to be the Devil's emissary to her' (*The Encyclopaedia of Witchcraft & Demonology*). It should also be remembered that Christianity didn't go 'green' until the late 20th century and therefore all wilderness places were the domain of the Devil and all old pastoral deities demonic.

However, as Nigel Jackson points out in *Call of the Horned Piper*, the Christian missionaries didn't have everything their own way, mistakenly thinking that if they converted the kings and tribal chieftains to the new religion, their control would filter down through the rank and file. Fortunately, the British have been remarkably tenuous when it comes to attempts at bull-dozing them into belief and it took until the Norman Conquest before Britain's ruling elite could be considered 'converted'.

In reality the intervening centuries would reveal that this process did not occur and that at the level of agrarian peasant life the pre-Christian lore and practices were adhered to tenaciously and boldly by the greater mass of rural folk. It simply proved impossible to eradicate the initiatic patterns of magical consciousness which were so deeply ingrained in the collective awareness of European country folk and which constituted an ancient oral inheritance of esoteric knowledge, mythopoetics and magical technologies.

Much of these Old Ways were cunningly concealed within traditional folklore, mumming and mystery plays, songs, dances and processions, agricultural customs and 'hidden' craft-associated practices (such as those of blacksmiths, shepherds, horsemen, midwives and wool-workers) that were slowly integrated into the early Church calendar so that Old Craft could be seen to be hiding in plain sight.

It became apparent by the medieval period that such deeply-rooted magical and religious forms, far from diminishing in occurrence, were actually flourishing and growing apace... The Old Faith, now under attack from above, receded further and further into the marginalised regions of society and persisted under a closer veil of secrecy than ever...the Craft of the Wise continued along hidden channels of transmission, often in old families in remote rural districts, in loose coven groupings, and in the lore of solitary Wyse-wives and Cunning-men.

The imported imagery of the witches' Horned God (usually Pan or satyr-like) appeared in wood-cuts and engravings in an attempt to terrify the uneducated through the medium of 'pamphlet literature'. Georg Luck, a classicist known for his studies of magical beliefs and practices in the Classical world, and for more than twenty years a professor at Johns Hopkins University, surprisingly endorsed some of Dr Margaret Murray's earlier theories. In *Arcana Mundi: Magic and the Occult in the Greek and Roman Worlds: A Collection of Ancient Texts* (1985) he stated that the Horned God may have appeared in late antiquity, stemming from the merging of Cernunnos, the antlered god of the Continental Celts, with the Greco-Roman Pan/Faunus, 'a combination of gods which created a new deity, around which the remaining pagans, those refusing to convert to Christianity, rallied and that this deity provided the prototype for later Christian conceptions of the devil, and his worshippers were cast by the Church as witches.'

Unlike the dense pine forests of northern Europe, Britain's climate was better suited to the softer, broad-leafed trees that evoked images of the pastoral setting of groves and idyllic woodland. Nevertheless, much of the 'real' Pan was lost in the translation from an all-powerful deity to a romantic, sylvan cipher. As Patricia Merivale observes:

> For most of the pre-Romantic Pans in English literature (and many thereafter), no Greek source need be supposed. Two stories from Ovid and a few lines from Virgil provided actions and attributes enough to fill the Elizabethan pastoral lyric and drama not only with icons of the pastoral scene but with lovesick Pans of many a vain pursuit and with Pans emblematic of such incompatibles as rustic ignorance and poetic creativity.

These romantic images are at odds with the anonymous nine-line Roman poem *Incerti ad Panem* that the presents Pan as unwashed, hairy, goatish, fierce, inconstant and noisy, '...an unusually frank glimpse at the logical result of postulating a god half-animal, in and of the countryside, and probably closer to the Pan that the Arcadians (or the Roman country-folk) actually believed in than the well scrubbed deity of Virgil.'

By contrast, Luca Signorelli's painting *The School of Pan* that the artist presented to Lorenzo de' Medici shows a youthful and sentimental god wearing a crescent moon on his head rather than horns. The painting was re-discovered in Florence c1870 and then sold to the Kaiser Frederick Museum in Berlin where it was subsequently destroyed by Allied bombs in WWII. The painting was almost the same as the one Luca painted on the wall of the Petrucci palace in Siena. In *Grasmere Lake* (1807), Great Pan is a voice rather than a vision, '...*the pipe was heard...thrilling the rocks/With tutelary music...low-whispering through the reeds...*' combining a naturalistic explanation of Pan's piping with a mythical explanation of the eerie sound of wind blowing through reeds. An example that tells us there is nothing to be seen of Pan apart from the natural objects that are his outer manifestations.

By the time Keats penned *Endymion*, Pan had manifested in all his glory and become a powerful thought-form as the *'Dread opener of the mysterious doors / Leading to [the] universal knowledge...'* that Eliphas Levi incorporated into the design of The Devil Tarot card Aleister Crowley included in the Thoth Tarot. In the hands of Dion Fortune, Arthur Machen and Aleister Crowley, Pan forcefully entered the realm of Western Ritual Magic and the genii was well and truly out of the bottle...

In 1930 Somerset Maugham looked back at what he saw as the 'Edwardian Pan cult' and commented: 'Thirty years ago in literary circles God was all the fashion...then God went out...and Pan came in. In a hundred novels his cloven hoof left its imprint on the sward; poets saw him lurking in the twilight...' Nevertheless, Pan who was once kept under control by the lofty Olympian gods and the Romans, bided his time:

> ...but equated with Satan by the Church, he became most mightily malignant; equated with sex, most basic and irresistible and, in some contexts, terrifying; equated with Greek civilisation and its culture, most humanistically lofty or paganly vigorous... Pan can represent the countryside as opposed to the city, a contrast not without intrinsic power even at its most trivial, for men have always wanted an escape from the world they have made for themselves such a Pan can be merely the touch of local colour...or he can be universal, transcendental Nature...

In the 1960s, the 'Celtic Twilight' began to seek out its own identity as followers of Wicca sought to remove the old Church names for the traditional festivals from the witches' Wheel of the Year, and introduced the old Gaelic Celtic names for the seasons despite the fact that Gaelic is the language of Ireland and Scotland. When Margaret Murray's *The God of the Witches* was published in 1933 she theorised that Pan was merely one form of a horned god who was worshipped across Europe by a witch-cult. This theory later influenced emerging Wiccan belief in viewing the archetype of the Horned God being represented by such deities as the Celtic Cernunnos and Greek Pan; despite the fact that clear evidence for the worship of Cernunnos has only been recovered on the European mainland, and not in Britain. Nevertheless, Dr Murray penned an Introduction to Gerald Gardner's *Witchcraft Today*, and the fantasy of her exaggeration of the 'organisational and congregational side of the Craft as a secret network' had begun.

A more appropriate 'deity' was later adopted in Herne the Hunter, a ghost associated with Windsor Forest, who was said to wear antlers upon his head. The first literary mention of Herne is in Shakespeare's play *The Merry Wives of Windsor*, though there have been several theories attempting to trace the origins of Herne as predating any actual evidence for him by connecting him to pagan deities or ancient archetypes. Herne, however, is a localised figure, not found outside Berkshire and the regions of the surrounding counties into which Windsor Forest once spread. In *The History of the Devil – The Horned God of the West Herne* (1929) R. Love Thompson suggested that Herne as well as other Wild Huntsmen in European folklore all derive from the same ancient source: 'My assumption is that these forms have been derived from the same Palæolithic ancestor and can, indeed, be regarded as two aspects of one central figure...' As a result some modern pagans accept Lowe Thompson's equation of Herne with Cernunnos, which they further connect to Pan (*Simple Wicca: A Simple Wisdom Book*). By the late 20th century, however, a number of scholars criticised the idea of these modern Celtic identities, sometimes also arguing that there never was a common Celtic culture, even in ancient times.

We are not saying that Pan *is* the Horned God, but with his impressive pedigree he stands as the embodiment of all horned gods; he is all things to all men – Pan Pangenetor – the

All-Begetter.

- He is the eternal personification of the pagan world – both ancient and modern;
- He is the god of all wild, untamed woodland and mountain slopes; and the guardian of Nature in all her guises;
- He is the archetypal lover and seducer, and the subject of a great deal of erotica as befits a fertility god;
- He has been the inspiration for countless works of art and literature from ancient Greek poets to the Edwardian novelists; from classic painted vases and sculptures to the paintings of the pre-Raphaelites;
- He provides us with a universally recognisable image that keeps alive the archaic culture of the Horned God however we choose to visualise him;
- He instilled panic into the heart of the Church – and emerged triumphant from the devilish oblivion to which they consigned him;
- He is fiercely protective towards his followers and, unlike many other focus of worship, *will* come when called upon;
- He links those Palaeolithic cave paintings and carvings created by our remote ancestors to present day anthropological theories and archaeological discoveries;
- He has powerful magical and mystical abilities – and may be a survivor of those hidden mystery cults that thrived in ancient Greece and Rome.

He is simply... Pan!

Possibly the greatest reluctance of modern pagans to pay homage to Pan as the Horned God, however, derives from the image created for the filming of *The Devil Rides Out* from the 1934 novel by Dennis Wheatley. The theme is one of 'black magic and devil worship' and in the Hammer House of Horror film version (1968), the sudden appearance of the Devil, complete with his goat's head and sitting Cernunnos-like on a mound, offended everyone with a serious affiliation to the Craft.

But this revulsion didn't apply to everyone. In an article for *Pop! Goes the Witch: The Disinformation Guide to 20th Century Witchcraft*, Caroline Tully wrote:

> One of my own favourite manifestations of the Horned God is Pan who reminds me that we are all animals – smart ones, but animals nevertheless. The ancient Greeks represented Pan as having the legs and horns of a goat but his appearance can actually range from that of a real goat standing upright, through to a man with a goatish face, human torso and goat legs, to a wholly human form sporting curved horns upon his head. A very popular deity in antiquity, Pan survived in medieval Europe as the goat-footed God of the Witches. The Christian church turned him into the Devil and the cloven hoof, once the sign of fertility and abundance, was regarded as evil. Anyone who has had much to do with real goats will know why they have a reputation as consorts of Witches. A buck goat looks like a man with a beard and wants to hump anything – including human females! Female readers, you might try going up to the fence next time you spy a billy-goat and see if he doesn't curl his lip in an epicurean fashion whilst inhaling your woman scent! It can be quite confronting for a city-dweller, but that's Nature in all her incomprehensible glory.

While in article for *White Dragon*, Anthony Roe wrote at length on 'The Great God Pan':

> As a schoolboy looking through the pages of *Picture Post*, I remember being curious about the reproductions of paintings from the walls of Aleister Crowley's Abbey in Sicily... In my youth I did not recognise Pan, the son of Hermes, the

Arcadian god of lust and magic who seduces men and women with his pipes and wantonness, the symbol of the libido in its sexual aspect, vagrant male sexuality, the personification of undisciplined procreation in nature. But the image remained with me, and I subsequently learnt that the herdsmen of ancient Greece adored Pan, and discovered the magick in connection with him... What was there about this frolicking god of the glen that made him so odious to the new Christians? Wherein was he Satanic? Perhaps in his sexual exploits. He is known to have seduced several nymphs. He also boasted that he had coupled with all Dionysus' drunken maenads. The episode related above wherein Pan seduces the Moon points to the Christian belief that Satan is able to disguise himself and seduce chaste women... It is in witchcraft that Pan – the symbol of Nature – still lives. His worship has ever lingered in field and fold.

So, thanks to the machinations of Christianity the devilish image of Pan has represented paganism in all varying its forms down through the ages. He became the archetypal figure for hedonism and licentiousness – often shown as some dreadful caricature of deviant lust, leering and ugly in his pursuit of beautiful nymphs who were repelled by his advances. By the Victorian and Edwardian Ages he was a character in the newly emerging horror fiction genre. Yet in the paintings of A W Bouguereau (1873) *Nymphs trying to teach Pan to dance* or Sir Edward Burne-Jones (1874) *Pan and Psyche,* we are transported back in time to Arcadia and reminded where this long journey first began.

To call upon Pan as the Dark Lord of the Forest and Horned God of the Witches, we can do no better than to use the opening lines of the *Orphic Hymn to Pan,* one of a collection of 87 short religious poems composed in either the late Hellenistic (3rd or 2nd century BC) or early Roman era. They are based on the beliefs of Orphism, a mystery cult or religious philosophy which claimed descent from the teachings of the mythical hero Orpheus and would have been heard when Pan was still being worshipped in his native land.

I call strong Pan, the substance of the whole,
Etherial, marine, earthly, general soul,
Immortal fire; for all the world is thine,
And all are parts of thee, O pow'r divine.

Come, blessed Pan, whom rural haunts delight,
Come, leaping, agile, wand'ring, starry light;
The Hours and Seasons, wait thy high command,
And round thy throne in graceful order stand.

Goat-footed, horned, Bacchanalian Pan,
Fanatic pow'r, from whom the world began,
Whose various parts by thee inspir'd, combine
In endless dance and melody divine.

Used as an invocation, the *Hymn* utilises the power of the elements and many of the facets of Pan's character, but it doesn't even have to be that verbose to call upon the Great God. In response to a post about Pan on Facebook, Anna Anima Mundi responded:

The most visceral ritual I've ever experienced happened during the Samhaintide eclipse of November 2003...someone spontaneously began chanting *'Io Pan'*, the rest of us picked it up, and He came. And partook. And didn't leave, really, for days... He left the fear behind, thankfully. He opened gates inside of us, and I am so grateful to have experienced that.

For those who practise their paganism in the safety of numbers, or behind closed doors, then perhaps there is much to be feared from this most ancient of gods; but for those who have grown up with Pan for a playmate, the reaction is probably more in keeping with his gentle compassion for Psyche. For Pan *is* all things to all who follow him – from the laughing pastoral deity to Pan Pangenetor, the cosmic All-Begetter. For all his complexity, however, once we've encountered Pan in his natural environment, our own response will probably be the same as that endearing little rodent from *The Wind in the Willows*: '*Afraid! Of Him? Oh, never, never! And yet – and yet – I am afraid!*'

Magical Exercise

If we truly wish to experience the 'Presence' we should try the following call taken from Aleister Crowley's *Hymn to Pan*, which has been used by all and sundry for years, simply because it works:

IO PAN! IO PAN!
IO PAN! PAN! PAN!
IO PAN! IO PAN!
IO PAN! PAN! PAN!

This refrain should be repeated over and over again when walking in the woods, timing each word to the rhythm of your step. Remember that the word 'panic' comes from Pan, so be prepared for an overwhelming sensation of fear. Nevertheless, the exercise can produce some very intense moments of Horned God energy!

Be warned: Do not call upon the Great God Pan unless you are prepared to encounter Him face to face when alone in the depths of the woods.

Other Names by Which Pan is Known

AEGO'CERUS (Aigokerôs): A surname of Pan, descriptive of his figure with the horns of a goat, but is more commonly the name given to one of the signs of the Zodiac. (Lucan, ix. 536; Lucret. v. 614; C. Caes. Germ. in Arat. 213.)

AGREUS (Agreus): A hunter, occurs as a surname of Pan and Aristaeus. (Pind. Pyth. ix. 115; Apollon. Rhod. iii. 507; Diod. iv. 81; Hesych. s.v.; Salmas. ad Solin. p. 81.)

LIMENI'TES, LIME'NIA, LIMENI'TIS, and LIMENO'SCOPUS (Limenia, Limenitês, Limenitis, Limenodkopos): Meaning the protector or superintendent of the harbour, occurs as a surname of several divinities, such as Zeus (Callimach. Fragm. 114, 2ded. Bentl.), Artemis (Callim. Hymn. in Dian. 259), Aphrodite (Paus. ii. 34. § 11; Serv. ad Aen. i. 724), Priapus (Anthol. Palat. x. 1, 7), and of Pan (Anthol. Palat. x. 10.)

LYTE'RIUS (Lutêrios): Meaning Deliverer, a surname of Pan, under which he had a sanctuary at Troezene, because he was believed during a plague to have revealed in dreams the proper remedy against the disease. (Paus. ii. 35. § 5.)

LYTIERSES (Lutiersês): Another form of Lityerses. (Theocr. x. 41.)

MAENA'LIUS or MAENA'LIDES (Mainalios): A surname of Pan, derived from mount Maenalus in Arcadia, which was sacred to the god. (Paus. viii. 26. § 2, 36. § 5; Ov. Fast. iv. 650.)

NO'MIUS (Noumios): A surname of divinities protecting the pastures and shepherds, such as Apollo, Pan. Hermes, and Aristaeus. (Aristoph. Thesmoph. 983; Anthol. Palat. ix. 217; Callim. Hymn. in Apoll. 47.)

Source: Dictionary of Greek and Roman Biography and Mythology.

The Orphic Hymns

These are a collection of 87 short religious poems dedicated to the individual Greek deities and composed in either the late Hellenistic (c3rd or c2nd BC) or early Roman (c1st to c2nd AD) era. They are based on the beliefs of Orphism, a mystery cult or religious philosophy, which claimed descent from the teachings of the mythical hero Orpheus.

A 1792 translation by Taylor with his notes is still available in print (*The Hymns of Orpheus* translated by Taylor, Thomas, 1792). A newer edition was published by University of Pennsylvania Press in 1999. However, a much more accurate, modern translation by A. Athanassakis has since been released (The Orphic Hymns, A. Athanassakis, Johns Hopkins University Press).

Source: www.theoi.com/Text/OrphicHymns1.html

Sources and Bibliography

The Age of Fable, Thomas Bulfinch (Harper and Row)

Arcana Mundi: Magic and the Occult in the Greek and Roman Worlds: A Collection of Ancient Texts, Georg Luck (Johns Hopkins University Press)

The Book of Thoth, Aleister Crowley (Weiser)

Call of the Horned Piper, Nigel Aldcroft Jackson (Capall Bann)

The Cultural Unconscious, Joseph L. Henderson (Jung Foundation)

The Encyclopaedia of Witchcraft & Demonology, Rossell Hope Robbins (Newnes)

Europe's Inner Demons, Norman Cohen (Paladin)

The Goat-Foot God, Dion Fortune (Aquarian)

The Gods of the Greeks, Karl Kerenyi (Thames & Hudson)

The Great God Pan, Arthur Machen (Keynote)

Haunted Greece: Nymphs, Vampires and Other Exotika, John L Tomkinson (Anagnosis)

Hecate's Fountain, Kenneth Grant (Skoob)

Herne the Hunter: A Berkshire Legend, Michael John Petry (WHS)

The Hollow Tree, Mélusine Draco (ignotus)

The Hymns of Orpheus, trans Thomas Taylor (UPP)

The Leaping Hare, George Ewart Evans (Faber)

The Lore of the Forest, Alexander Porteous (Senate)

Magic in the Middle Ages, Richard Kieckhefer (CUP)

The Magical Revival, Kenneth Grant (Skoob)

Malleus Malleficarum, ed. Pennethorne Hughes (Folio)

Malleus Satani, Suzanne Ruthven (ignotus)

Man, Myth & Magic, ed Richard Cavendish (Cavendish)

Modern Greek Folklore & Ancient Greek Religion, John Cuthbert Lawson (Forgotten Books)

The Oxford Companion to Classical Literature, Ed. Sir Paul Harvey (OUP)

Pan the Goat God: His Myth in Modern Times, Patricia Merivale

(Harvard UP)

The Power of Images, David Freedberg (Chicago)

Religion and the Decline of Magic, Keith Thomas (Weidenfeld & Nicholson)

Roman Britain, T W Potter and Catherine Johns (BMP)

The Roman Festivals of the Period of the Republic, Warde W Fowler (MacMillan)

The Religion of Ancient Rome, Cyril Bailey (OUP)

Root & Branch: British Magical Tree Lore, Mélusine Draco (ignotus)

Sex, Dissidence and Damnation, Jeffery Richards (Routledge)

Simple Wicca: A Simple Wisdom Book, Michele Morgan (Conari)

Traditional Witchcraft & the Pagan Revival, Mélusine Draco (Moon Books)

Viral Mythology, Marie D Jones and Larry Flaxman (New Page)

The Wind in the Willows, Kenneth Grahame (Folio)

The Winged Bull, Dion Fortune

Witchcraft Today, Gerald Gardner (Magical Childe)

About the Author

Mélusine Draco originally trained in the magical arts of traditional British Old Craft with Bob and Mériém Clay-Egerton. She has been a magical and spiritual instructor for more than 20 years with Coven of the Scales and the Temple of Khem, and writer of numerous popular books. Her highly individualistic teaching methods and writing draws on ancient sources supported by academic texts and current archaeological findings; believing that magic is an amalgam of science and art, and that magic is the outer route to the inner Mysteries. She now lives in Ireland near the Galtee Mountains and has several titles currently published with John Hunt Publishing including the Traditional Witchcraft series; two titles on totem animals – *Aubry's Dog* and *Black Horse, White Horse*; *By Spellbook & Candle: Hexing, Cursing, Bottling & Binding* and *The Secret People: Parish-pump witchcraft, Wise-women and Cunning Ways* published by Moon Books; in additional to *Magic Crystals Sacred Stones* and *The Atum-Re Revival* published by Axis Mundi Books.

Website:
http://www.covenofthescales.com
Website:
http://www.templeofkhem.com
Blog:
http://melusinedracoattempleofkhem.blogspot.com/
Facebook:
https://www.facebook.com/Melusine-Draco-486677478165958
Facebook:
http://www.facebook.com/TradBritOldCraft
Facebook:
http:// www.facebook.com/TempleofKhem
Facebook:
http://www.facebook.com/TempleHouseArchive

MOON
BOOKS

Moon Books

PAGANISM & SHAMANISM

What is Paganism? A religion, a spirituality, an alternative
belief system, nature worship? You can find support for all
these definitions (and many more) in dictionaries,
encyclopaedias, and text books of religion, but subscribe to
any one and the truth will evade you. Above all Paganism is a
creative pursuit, an encounter with reality, an exploration of
meaning and an expression of the soul. Druids, Heathens,
Wiccans and others, all contribute their insights and literary
riches to the Pagan tradition. Moon Books invites you to begin
or to deepen your own encounter, right here, right now.
If you have enjoyed this book, why not tell other readers by
posting a review on your preferred book site. Recent
bestsellers from Moon Books are:

Journey to the Dark Goddess
How to Return to Your Soul
Jane Meredith
Discover the powerful secrets of the Dark Goddess and
transform your depression, grief and pain into healing
and integration.
Paperback: 978-1-84694-677-6 ebook: 978-1-78099-223-5

Shamanic Reiki
Expanded Ways of Working with Universal Life Force Energy
Llyn Roberts, Robert Levy
Shamanism and Reiki are each powerful ways of healing;
together, their power multiplies. Shamanic Reiki introduces
techniques to help healers and Reiki practitioners tap ancient
healing wisdom.
Paperback: 978-1-84694-037-8 ebook: 978-1-84694-650-9

Pagan Portals - The Awen Alone
Walking the Path of the Solitary Druid
Joanna van der Hoeven
An introductory guide for the solitary Druid, *The Awen Alone*
will accompany you as you explore, and seek out your own
place within the natural world.
Paperback: 978-1-78279-547-6 ebook: 978-1-78279-546-9

A Kitchen Witch's World of Magical Herbs & Plants
Rachel Patterson
A journey into the magical world of herbs and plants, filled with
magical uses, folklore, history and practical magic. By popular
writer, blogger and kitchen witch, Tansy Firedragon.
Paperback: 978-1-78279-621-3 ebook: 978-1-78279-620-6

The Medicine for the Soul
Complete Book of Shamanic Healing
Ross Heaven
All you will ever need to know about shamanic healing and
how to become your own shaman...
Paperback: 978-1-78099-419-2 ebook: 978-1-78099-420-8

Shaman Pathways - The Druid Shaman
Exploring the Celtic Otherworld
Danu Forest
A practical guide to Celtic shamanism with exercises and
techniques as well as traditional lore for exploring the Celtic
Otherworld.
Paperback: 978-1-78099-615-8 ebook: 978-1-78099-616-5

Traditional Witchcraft for the Woods and Forests
A Witch's Guide to the Woodland with Guided Meditations and
Pathworking
Melusine Draco
A Witch's guide to walking alone in the woods, with guided
meditations and pathworking.
Paperback: 978-1-84694-803-9 ebook: 978-1-84694-804-6

Wild Earth, Wild Soul
A Manual for an Ecstatic Culture
Bill Pfeiffer
Imagine a nature-based culture so alive and so connected,
spreading like wildfire. This book is the first flame...
Paperback: 978-1-78099-187-0 ebook: 978-1-78099-188-7

Naming the Goddess
Trevor Greenfield
Naming the Goddess is written by over eighty adherents and
scholars of Goddess and Goddess Spirituality.
Paperback: 978-1-78279-476-9 ebook: 978-1-78279-475-2

Shapeshifting into Higher Consciousness
Heal and Transform Yourself and Our World with Ancient
Shamanic and Modern Methods
Llyn Roberts
Ancient and modern methods that you can use every day

to transform yourself and make a positive difference in the world.

Paperback: 978-1-84694-843-5 ebook: 978-1-84694-844-2

Readers of ebooks can buy or view any of these bestsellers by clicking on the live link in the title. Most titles are published in paperback and as an ebook. Paperbacks are available in traditional bookshops. Both print and ebook formats are available online.

Find more titles and sign up to our readers' newsletter at http://www.johnhuntpublishing.com/paganism. Follow us on Facebook at https://www.facebook.com/MoonBooks and Twitter at https://twitter.com/MoonBooksJHP.